TED ELLIS

The People's Naturalist

TED ELLIS

The People's Naturalist

Eugene Stone

JARROLD COLOUR PUBLICATIONS, NORWICH

Frontispiece: Ted Ellis at Wheatfen in 1968

ISBN 0-7117-0436-8
© 1988 Jarrold Colour Publications
Printed and Published in Great Britain by Jarrold & Sons Ltd, Norwich 1/88

Contents

Foreword by Timothy Colman *page* 7

Acknowledgements 8

1 **From Guernsey with love** 9

2 **Yarmouth, a new habitat** 21

3 **Old Father William and other friends** 36

4 **The museum years** 48

5 **The war years** 66

6 **A home on the fen** 75

7 **Home life** 96

8 **Rusts and smuts** 117

9 **Putting pen to paper** 129

10 **A freelance takes wing** 133

11 **The legacy** 152

Postscript by Phyllis Ellis 157

The Ted Ellis Trust 158

Foreword

This book will bring great pleasure to all who seek enlightenment from the simple beauties of nature. It is a human narrative full of anecdote, and told in a natural and easy style. It captures the life of an exceptional man who was not only a brilliant naturalist, but at the same time a natural communicator.

In the title, Ted Ellis has been aptly described as the people's naturalist. It is a compliment he deserves. Those who were privileged to know him will identify easily with many of the events recounted and the warm personality portrayed. But this biography will also inspire a wider audience through succeeding generations.

From the earliest days of his childhood in Guernsey to the fullness of his life in the county of Norfolk, from which he never allowed himself to be tempted away, Ted Ellis meticulously observed and recorded the smallest events in the natural world.

He 'hath the eyes of a falcon and the optimism of a Sancho Panza,' wrote Arthur Patterson, the celebrated Yarmouth naturalist. But throughout a long life of achievement he also kept the enviable gift of being a listener, never too proud to talk with and learn from anyone he met. It didn't matter if you were young or old, expert or ignorant. Whether you were reading his regular column in the local newspaper, sharing some discovery on television, or peering beside him into a dyke at his beloved Wheatfen, the feeling was the same. He was simply himself whilst you were the most important member of his audience. You could not but feel enriched by the experience.

For this delightful biography, we are indebted to the author, who has captured so successfully the many facets of an exceptionally attractive, enthusiastic and talented personality, revealing the naturalist, writer, broadcaster and poet, and passing on the nuggets of practical wisdom which appear throughout these pages.

To the question, 'How is it that there are not more naturalists?' Ted Ellis had a ready answer, 'Grown-ups arrange too many other activities for the young.'

Timothy Colman

Acknowledgements

To make this book possible, many friends of Ted have given generously of their time and reminiscences. I would like to thank them all for, in different ways, helping me to build up a picture of a man who defies description and lives more richly in their memories than my words can describe. I am grateful to Mr Timothy Colman, Lady Enid Ralphs, Mr Harry Last, Mr John Mountford, Mr Gordon Moseley, Mr Doug Salmon, Mr Percy Trett, Dr Joyce Lambert, Dr Tony Irwin, Mr John Goldsmith, Mr Bob Driscoll, Dr A. Batty-Shaw, Mr Malcolm Freegard, Dr Roy Baker, Mr Keith Clarke, Mrs Sue Hall, the Reverend Kit Chalcraft, Mr Tim Peet, Mr George Robinson, Mr Brian Fawcett, Mrs Elizabeth Loy, Mr Alan Watson, Professor Arthur Hunter, Mrs J. M. Clayton, Mr Tim Wyatt, Mr Peter Orton, Mr Keith Clement and Mrs Ruth Race.

All the members of Ted's family have assisted me. So thanks, too, to Suzie, Lucy, John, Mary, Martin, the older Martin, Ted's brother, to Colin Stiff, Bobby Hanna . . . and above all, to Phyllis.

I am also grateful to Beryl Tooley for permission to quote from her biography of her great-grandfather, *John Knowlittle*, published in 1985 by Wilson-Poole; and to the BBC for permission to use unpublished material – they sent a reporter to talk with Ted in his final weeks and taped a conversation.

Ted did not live to write the autobiography that he often talked about. However, he had told more of his own story, over the years, than perhaps he realised and so I have been able to quote his own words at many points, taking them from various sources but especially from his 'In the Country-side' and 'Young Naturalist' articles for the *Eastern Daily Press*.

Eugene Stone

1 ❧ From Guernsey with love

When I was a child I had a favourite wild flower. It was the centaury, a rather small, tufted plant with heads of bright rose-pink starry flowers, which I knew then on the cliff turf of the Channel Islands. When the flowers were fully open in warm sunshine they had a matchless fragrance which was too delicate for grown-ups to detect. To me it was the precious spikenard, sweeter even than the scent of gorse in May.

Ted Ellis was born at St Sampson, Guernsey on 22 May 1909 and, as that first summer lengthened into autumn, it was a new beginning for all the family. Alice, his mother, was thirty-eight years old and had been widowed in 1900 with a son of ten days. Struggling to bring him up alone, she worked as a school-teacher in Yarmouth, sharing her grand-parents' home and looking after them until their death. It was in Yarmouth that she met and married James Ellis, a colourful wanderer with a fine silver-baritone voice . . . and a fierce temper. As a youth, 'Jimmy' had run away from an apprenticeship in his wealthy father's tailoring firm, fleeing first to London, then crossing America and Canada as a singer and piano player. Finally, he had returned home seeking quieter days.

They came to the temperate island on honeymoon, and decided to stay. Guernsey was . . .

a rugged island, with precipitous cliffs and hundreds of bays. Standing out of the sea, which was so clear that the sun cast deep purple, green and blue lights in it, were great stacks of rock, where thousands of seabirds wheeled and screamed and congregated to breed. Shoals of mackerel and grey mullet going by used to appear like dark cloud-shadows in the water. Green meadows topped the land, and wild furze brakes, pine forests, tracts of heather and wild thyme, where rabbits gambolled, sloped to the shore. Various little ferns, sea pinks, and sea lavender cropped out of the cliff faces.

So Ted remembered it. Those rocks were the notorious Pea Stacks — sheer, jagged columns rising out of the sea with violent waves seething between them. By the time he was old enough to notice, there were often two tiny figures balanced precariously on the windy tops, gathering gulls' eggs.

The intrepid scavengers were his half-brother Percy, a large, loud and jolly boy, and Percy's boyhood friend Bert Crocker. In the enthusiasm of their hunting, this pair would lay planks across the dizzy drops and wobble their way from one Stack to another.

Percy, aged nine, was already a huge figure. He would swing the new, laughing baby up onto his shoulders and, before long, was taking him swimming on his back far out around the Point. He was Ted's first hero. But according to family tradition, as the young Ted began to experiment in his own way — early — with childish language, there was a strange omen of the future. He had already spoken a few, separate words . . . 'Mama', 'Dada', but had never put them together. One day, he surprised Alice. As she stood over his pram, a fly settled on the cover and his tiny voice piped, BOLD INSECT!

Guernsey was a paradise — but it was a long way from home. The Ellis family trace their ancestry back through burghers and Members of Parliament in Yarmouth (including French Huguenot settlers of the Beazer-Blois family) to the thirteenth century, originally spelling their name 'Elys', the Norfolk way. And, though Ted was the family's first naturalist, Elizabeth Postle of East Runton, Norfolk, a renowned 'wise woman' of the early 1800s, known for her herbal cures, was his father's grandmother. Alice, born in 1871, had a successful Yarmouth silversmith for a father — George Archard of King Street.

Alice and Jimmy named their son Edward Augustine, preserving a family tradition; Augustin, though without the final 'e', was his father's middle name, and had been passed down from the time of Elizabeth Postle's father. But perhaps the greatest gift they gave him was liberty. With the cursory precaution of a red sweater — so that he would be visible at a distance — Alice let him run wild over the cliffs and countryside. He favoured that colour all his life — perhaps through association — and still had several red pullovers in old age!

> In the beginning I was able to adventure freely in the wildest of settings, scrambling over the flowery cliffs of Guernsey, watching soaring sea birds, hovering kestrels, croaking ravens, swarms of butterflies, ferocious ants, weird bugs and beetles, and discovering a wealth of marine life in caves and rock pools when the tides were out.

Soon he was joined by an equally adventurous younger brother, Martin. Born in 1911, he shared Ted's enthusiasm. Before long he was sharing the red sweaters as well.

A picture taken of a laughing, two-year-old Ted at that time — in a Guernsey bonnet — brought him his first, early, national appearance. It was sent by the local doctor, who snapped it, to Wellington Cameras. Impressed

Top left: Ted at just nine months, a picture taken by his father. *Top right:* the award-winning smile snapped by the local doctor. *Bottom:* a one-year-old already exploring the garden, another of Jimmy's pictures

by that eye-catching smile, they used it in a popular advertisement poster of the early 1900s — and so the public had its first glimpse of the famous naturalist. In time, the company disappeared but, on the wall of the BBC's Elstree Studios in London, the poster was preserved by someone who liked its image of an unknown captivating child. Nobody could have been more startled to see it than Ted . . . when he made his first broadcast there in the early 1950s! It shows a child full of joy in life . . . for whom the world contains magic. And for Ted it certainly did . . .

> I was already familiar with a rich assortment of things like sea anemones, barnacles, limpets, dog whelks, jellyfish and even an octopus observed in a rock pool. I had marvelled at my first glimpse of peacock butterflies and a green lizard basking on a rock on the same unforgettable day. I watched nesting gulls, cormorants, ravens and puffins from precipices whenever I could slip away unnoticed. I knew the catlike smell of early purple orchids growing among the bluebells, the heavenly fragrance of the small pink centaury and thrift on the cliffs.

In those first years . . .

> There were zebra beetles, bloody-nosed beetles, aphids smothering red campions, a nest of young robins overrun by large ferocious ants, a wren that died of terror between my small, cupped hands when I plucked it out of an ivy bush out of sheer wonder and curiosity.

Ted remembered that dying wren all his life, telling friends that it taught him 'to be gentle with all wild creatures'. For both brothers, the early adventures lasted. Martin was to become a successful scientist in his own right — also a fungus specialist, eventually becoming chief mycologist at the Commonwealth Mycological Institute at Kew.

But for now there was much to learn. Lessons at the tiny Board School were half in English, half in French — though different again, he noticed, was the French patois spoken locally by many islanders. Ted's lifelong interest in the preservation of Norfolk dialect had its early inspiration in those foreign sounds. On the way home from school the boys would stop at old Mrs Wise's shop for a bag of humbugs — which could be bought for a 'double', an eighth of an old penny — or he would buy 'tiger nuts'. They were a favourite of Ted's and set him a delicious mystery that took half a lifetime to solve. What were they? 'These so-called "nuts" were like grubby little roots usually hard and often gritty; but their sweet flavour made up for these deficiencies. I never knew what they were precisely.' An older Ted went on wondering but found no answer in any of his reference books. Then, at last, in 1961 he found his boyhood delicacy again, much cleaner now and wrapped in cellophane, but recognisable. With the eye of experience, he identified 'the tubers of a sedge — *Cyperus esculentus* — closely related to our

Elegantly dressed for a pre-war studio portrait, the Ellis family with Ted *(front)* aged three, and Martin and Percy *(back)*. Some of Alice's needlework can be seen displayed on the youngsters' cuffs and collars

13

English galingale and the papyrus of the ancient Egyptians.' That day, in triumph, he devoted his regular newspaper article to tiger nuts!

On the road home from school Ted also collected snails and caterpillars, characteristically taking note of what they were eating, so that they could be reared on the right plants. His bedroom contained a mass of decaying cabbage leaves, which Alice tracked down by the smell! They were food for his pet caterpillars. Soon he was doing more than collecting them; he was breeding them — to see what they would turn into — in little glass jars all over the house, each capped with a piece of paper pierced with holes. It was a fascination that started on his very doorstep . . .

> I was introduced to caterpillars at the age of three, helping my father to pick those of the large white butterfly from cabbage leaves for a small reward which went into my money box.

He received a halfpenny for every twenty but this was not enough to stop him being overcome with remorse when he found that his captives were subjected to drowning in salt water! From that day, he began to save just a few as pets. Ted looked closely, and missed little. Soon he was led — in the interests of scientific enquiry — to chewing flowers! He had seen the identical caterpillars 'eating leaves of nasturtiums which surprised me until I discovered that they tasted very much like some cabbages and cresses.' Other varieties of caterpillar quickly joined his collection, and a lifetime's sense of wonder was awakened . . .

> I found that some kinds spun silken cocoons on the plants when full grown while others went into the ground to pupate. Sometimes the expected perfect butterflies or moths failed to appear; instead, parasitic wasps or flies emerged from the chrysalids in which they had lived as parasites.
>
> I also discovered that some of my insects failed to spread their wings properly when coming out of the chrysalids and remained crumpled and crippled unless they could climb to a point where their newly formed wings could expand as fluid was pumped into them during a slow process before they were fully stretched and lost their initial limpness.

Some of the lessons were more harsh — as when the delighted child discovered a nest of baby robins and rushed home for breadcrumbs to feed them. Having done so he returned later for another peek. There his pleasure turned to horror as he looked at dead chicks which had been savagely attacked and eaten alive by carnivorous ants. Even to a child it was obvious what had led the ants to the well-hidden babies — Ted's breadcrumbs. The ghastly sense of guilt left him with a lifelong conviction that naïve humans can do great harm by interfering with birds' nests. Even in his old age Ted did not universally welcome bird-watchers to his home, though he made exceptions of trusted individuals. The gruesome moment also left the man who loved nature with a little-known phobia of ants. 'I have an uncomfort-able feeling . . . almost a dread of them,' he once said.

The family were living at St Martin's when Ted's brother was born. Later they moved to Jerbourg where his mother ran a successful tea garden and sold delicate water-colour paintings to the tourists. Though no naturalist, Jimmy had a large garden wherever they lived. He was, in fact, far more than a gardener; he bred chickens and other livestock, and kept detailed notebooks on the progress of everything he grew . . . recording how many eggs were laid, writing up experiments with tree-grafting, noting obser-vations on plant diseases. Jimmy regularly took *The Smallholder* magazine. Never employed, and always independently minded, he regarded himself as a gentleman.

Ted did not get on well with his father and, in later years, claimed that any talent he had came from Alice; clearly, though, that was unfair. Jimmy was a sociable man, living — precariously — on a fixed income from investments. He entertained his sons with comic songs like *I Want A Wife Not An Ornament,* accompanying himself boisterously on the piano. And he taught them his maxim: 'Always remember you are no better than any other man — and no worse!'

Alice was a motherly, kind woman — later a favourite with Ted's own children — who had a great love of the countryside and was artistic. In her paintings and in beautifully detailed embroidery landscapes she certainly showed the keen eye and near photographic recall that Ted was to inherit. Often she would sketch just a few lines of a scene in chalk and then — over the weeks — add all the rich colour and form of trees, flowers and reeds from memory, her stitching skilfully bending the grasses to the direction of the breeze. She fostered their love of art and nature, made them prize-winning fancy dress costumes and read to them . . .

> Here we go, all the way,
> Up the stairs to blanket bay!

This rhyme, heard 'at mother's knee', was one of Ted's earliest memories. And in bed there were stories . . .

> I took a great delight in reading and having read to me the adventures of a naughty little mouse called Scribble-Scrabble who, in the story, popped out of a hole in the skirting every night and was watched at his antics by two children, in candle-light. In secret, they supplied him with toasted cheese and other morsels, while parents frowned at the evidence of Scribble-Scrabble's doings and set traps which the children, of course, sprang so that no harm should befall their sprightly visitor.

As Ted listened, the nights were deepened by the strange cawing of rooks in the treetops. 'What's in the dark?' he asked his mother. 'The birds seemed to be holding strange conversations and to be bidding a mournful farewell to the day, and I found it very awe-inspiring and thrilling to listen to their gloomy gossip; they were like a lot of winged black goblins belonging to a world of make-believe. I would have liked to join them in their tree-top lookouts under the stars and to have learnt their language.'

What's in the dark, mother? 'Sixty years later,' he wrote . . . 'I still wonder!'

The spell of early story-telling took hold, too. Ted, in private, became a gifted improviser of tales, entertaining his brother Martin, from their earliest years right into their teens, with his inventions. Every night there would be a story. 'Very often he would stop as I started to fall asleep,' Martin recalls, 'and it would be continued the next night, developing into a long serial.' Ted would humorously weave in real people, adding spice — and occasionally scandal — to the tale. When his grandchildren were old enough to understand, the tradition began again, and they too were introduced to the magical world of his fairy tales and yarns . . . stories like:

MISS TINCANNY AND THE BONG

Miss Tincanny was small and prim. She lived in a villa standing by itself in a shrubbery and was looked after by an apple-cheeked old woman and a large magical dog named the Bong. Miss Tincanny visited a different friend every afternoon and always stayed out for tea. She wore a tight-waisted sealskin coat winter and summer, and a black velvet tam o'shanter with a bright blue feather in it.

She never took the Bong visiting, in case he did anything magical, and no-one knew of her secret possession. To everyone, she was just a friendly, gossip-ing, old-fashioned body. Then one day Miss Tincanny caught a chill and had to stay at home for a whole month. She sent little notes to all her regular friends explaining why she couldn't come to tea as usual, and begging them not to call on her.

After a week had gone by, however, her friends plucked up courage to go and ask after her health, and by chance seven of them arrived together at three o'clock on Saturday afternoon. One rang the bell. The door was opened at once, to their astonishment, by a large black dog which vanished as soon as they looked at it . . .

And, in the only written version, Ted's tale vanishes there, too. Perhaps it is fitting that if we want any more . . . we will have to invent it ourselves!

Long before natural history figured in any of his lessons at school, Ted was hearing tales — from Alice — of her grandfather, who had gone to sea on the whaling ships. And he was even learning from sets of cigarette cards, including one entitled 'The struggle for existence', which vividly impressed upon him, even at that early age, the ideas of Charles Darwin. He was sent to

Sunday School and there also — in the church cemetery — he found natural history lessons . . .

> I came upon a glittering bronze and gold chrysalis, which proved to be that of a small tortoiseshell butterfly, tucked into an overhang of a wall. On another occasion I was fascinated by the perfect, lichen-like camouflage of marbled beauty moths settled on the granite masonries of a church porch. Emerging from a morning service one day, I caught sight of some gorgeous caterpillars: black, with scarlet and white ornamentation on a little copper plum tree near the entrance. In the turf nearby I found my first four-leaved clover.
>
> On the flat tops of family vaults there were often scattered shells of brightly coloured banded snails, smashed there by thrushes. Many of the old grave-stones were strangely patterned with lichens, mostly on one side. I noticed birds collecting confetti and other paper oddments strewing the paths after weddings, to use in nest building.

His father's compost heap was equally fascinating. There he discovered seedling date palms sprouting . . . and talked his father into transferring some of them to pots in his greenhouse, where they flourished. At the age of five, he was also planting experimental seeds in Jimmy's garden — though a little impatiently at first: 'I dug them up after a few days to see if they were really any good. When little sprouts were showing, they had to be buried again quickly!'

With Jimmy and Alice both busy at home, there was often time made for a picnic on a fine day. And every autumn the whole family would go black-berrying, collecting enough to make 100 lb of jam, which would be poured into rows and rows of jars . . . and fed to the visitors all summer.

Ted and Martin became 'explorers', too, and 'Red Indians' as they roamed the woods — making camps, carving mysterious signs on the trees and once renaming a tiny trickle of a stream (from TEd and MArtin) as the mighty 'Tema' River. The young naturalist's Indian name was 'Taquame-naw' and twenty years later he was still able to find where he had carved it on a small holm oak during one of his boyhood games.

There was also time for mischief! Ted did his share of invading orchards, swopping garden gates, and, where the cliff path ran by at rooftop height, placing turf over chimney-pots with sudden smoky results for the inhabi-tants! One special day, Ted and boyhood pal Alfie Frampton, a fisherman's son, discovered a treasure trove of boxes and bottles washed up on the beach after a storm. It contained such delights as port wine, and toffee. They smuggled the lot into Alfie's loft and gorged themselves . . . to emerge some time later, happily, stickily drunk!

Another friend, Denny, shared his interest in insects . . .

> Denny had various caterpillars in hand, including a young one of a lobster moth in which we were both keenly interested. Denny's mother couldn't do

with insects on the premises, however, and accordingly the caterpillars — coming by chance under her observation — were thrown out. Denny told me of this and, in vengeance, I remember packing a great many woodlice and earwigs in a cardboard box, wrapping it up in brown paper, addressing it to his mother, sticking some used stamps thereon, and delivering it surreptitiously at the front door. The trick did not come off, however, as Denny was told to unpack the parcel; I shouldn't wonder if his mother, always with a guarded eye, had some suspicions.

If ideas for mischief were lacking, Ted's older half-brother Percy could always be relied on for inspiration. Not content with the hazards of bridging the Pea Stacks, in another escapade he discovered that kestrels were nesting half-way up a sheer, inaccessible cliff. Percy had only a little box camera, but he was determined to get a picture of the young. So he achieved the same effect as modern telephoto lenses . . . but more directly: he was lowered, inch by inch, down the cliff on a rope by a sweating, straining team of schoolboy chums. The twelve-year-old got his pictures. They even came out! He had a streak of luck in proportion to his nerve and did, once, tumble over the cliffs . . . only to be pulled up by his braces!

The family's independent life-style gave them a virtually hand-to-mouth existence, but Jimmy was enterprising. He sold garden produce, bred rabbits, and soon added quite a large herd of goats which he tethered on the cliff-tops. Ted and Martin helped to tend them and were rewarded with rides in a little carriage drawn, alternately, by a passive white nanny and a less amiable little brown goat with sharp horns. Then one day the herd was joined by a massive, bearded, curly-horned billy. This fierce and lordly mountain goat was the mascot of the Welsh Fusiliers. The soldiers were now bound for the trenches of France, where they could not take him, and from which many of them would never return.

Jimmy was pulled back from the brink of disaster on the eve of the First World War; he was planning his most ambitious scheme to make (or break) the family's fortunes — by sinking all of their savings and invested capital into the purchase of a large hotel. Success would depend on tourism but the war was to end tourism for four years. As Jimmy was about to settle the deal, a local bank manager — who was a personal friend — warned him that the declaration was expected.

So, instead, the family shut up their tea garden and moved to a large, rented house at St Jacques. There, Jimmy had his most extensive garden. He bred chickens of many varieties, rearing the chicks in artificial hatcheries warmed by paraffin lamps. . . as Ted and Martin sat, fascinated, listening to life tapping its way out of the shell. He also continued to breed several types of rabbit for their meat and fur. The garden had every conceivable variety of fruit tree or bush — apples, pears, raspberries, strawberries, blackcurrants,

Ted, aged six, and Martin, already close friends with nature — these baby goats from their father's herd were familiar playmates

gooseberries. There was a huge fig tree, a well-established vine, a tomato house, and a wide range of vegetables. Jimmy started a weekly produce stall in the French-style covered market at St Peter Port, with his sons helping to man it.

The owner of the St Jacques house — another of Jimmy's friends — was the local cinema manager. So there were sometimes free tickets for Ted and Martin . . . and, in the dark, they got to know the early silent movie stars — Charlie Chaplin, Pearl White and many others. The 'Westerns', however, were their favourites.

During the closing months of the war Jimmy and Alice concluded, reluctantly, that with too few jobs available there was little future for their growing sons on the island. Percy, lying about his age, had joined the Navy in 1915. The rest of the family, too, now made plans for a new start and their decision to leave Guernsey brought to a close what Ted often called the happiest time in his life. With a flora and fauna characteristic of a warmer climate (until he was ten Ted had only once seen snow), Guernsey was a very different place from their new destination — Norfolk. Yet it was here that the course had been set which was to make him the great naturalist of the fenlands.

I am often asked 'How does one begin to be a naturalist? Just by living in the country when you are small enough, isn't it'? Looking back, I'm sure that nearly all the little boys and girls I played with and walked round the fields, lanes, woods, cliffs and beaches with were curious about flowers, caterpillars, snails, crabs and seaweeds. Some of us were encouraged by our parents and grown-up friends, and by older children who knew more than we did about the names of things. Others were not so lucky.

One of my friends had a kind father who helped him to set his butterflies, and in later life he became an expert entomologist. In my own case, I remember with gratitude two young pupil-teachers who let me accompany them on a dragonfly hunt in some watermeadows when I was still so small that the long grass seemed high enough to get lost in. I also think of a red-letter day when an older boy, spending a holiday near my home, asked me if I would like to see some lady's tresses orchids in a field; the beauty and scent of these little white flowers on twisted spikes in the grass thrilled me tremendously.

Then there was the military man who used to go for long cross-country walks with his dog; he stopped to talk one day and told me the way to a wild rhododendron bush in flower.

We begin very simply looking at the life about us. We hunt creatures . . . we pick flowers. If people are kind and quick to share their fuller knowledge, we can go on being naturalists. I think the proper question to ask should be 'How is it that there are not more naturalists?' I know the answer to this one: grown-ups arrange too many other activities for the young.

2 ❧ Yarmouth, a new habitat

ed never lost the enchantment with Guernsey; he returned there nine times for holidays — the last in 1985 — and once considered retiring there. He was ten years old when their boat pulled away.

The first thing to arouse my curiosity on approaching the shores of England in June 1920 was a coarse grass growing along the muddy fringe of Southampton Water as we steamed into harbour. There were vast beds of it, half flooded at the time, and they seemed to me then a strange kind of bulwark against the sea after my previous experience of rocky shores and great tides besetting them.

The family came to Norfolk — staying at first with the village school-mistress in Hopton (then still part of Suffolk), Ted's Aunt Ethel. Soon they bought a small, terraced house in Springfield Road, Gorleston, and Jimmy consoled himself by taking an allotment. For Ted, too, it had meant leaving more behind than old friends . . .

flat countryside, sandy cliffs where I had been used to these rocky precipices, marshes — thousands of acres of flat marshland! The Broads, rivers, estuaries . . . a totally new world.

At first he was despondent. Outside he could see only a concrete break-water, the pavements of a marine parade, and the stone and brickwork of buildings. But soon . . .

I was exploring the footpaths, walking round the banks of the estuaries and absorbing the character and variety of a new kind of wildlife, new flowers, new birds and, of course, I was always interested in the minutiae — snails, beetles, little insects creeping in the grass.

And on closer inspection even those walls and pavements became interesting . . .

There were still plants sprouting from crevices, lichens, mosses and algae whose growth was most encouraged in damp and shady situations, while insects, spiders, mites and well-camouflaged moths were also part of the scene.

These were to be the years when Ted gained confidence and, in a decade, grew from a keen youngster into a recognised authority. Soon he knew, and was using, every footpath within ten miles of Yarmouth . . . following them into Norfolk's marshes, estuaries, little commons and parish pits, often covering twenty miles in a day on foot. He didn't even have a bicycle yet!

The summer of his first real explorations, 1921, was an unusually fine one . . . and nature had its own way of marking the date, in celebration of the long months of sunshine. An especially broad growth ring was left for Ted to discover, long after, on ash trees flourishing in a damp part of Wheatfen . . . by then his home. 'The pattern of the years is imprinted in trees so faithfully that we are able to learn quite a lot about the weather of bygone times,' he wrote.

When he ventured into the lanes, he found them peaceful, rutted by cart-wheels and pitted by the hooves of horses, for as yet 'motorcars were something of a novelty, appearing rather like dragons as their progress, even at a mere 20–30 miles an hour, was marked by clouds of dust on summer days.' He roamed, collecting specimens and taking notes, and drew strangers to him by his enthusiasm.

> I met many interesting old people out in the country; because they were old, they had time to talk, and they told me interesting things about birds and other animals and the uses of various wild herbs. There were also game-keepers, wildfowlers, anglers, and occasionally tramps and gypsies; all open-air people who shared my pleasures in one way or another.

Even the town ratcatcher became one of his teachers!

In Ted's early years, as there were few natural history books available, he could not always discover the names of things he found. But his brother Martin recalls how, undeterred, Ted would still make little sketches and descriptions of the flower or insect, noting where it had been seen, what was associated with it . . . everything he could discover, to keep as a reminder. As Ted later wrote:

> I was storing up wonderful memories of creatures I had stopped to watch and exciting wild flowers I had chanced upon. I could enjoy the beauty of a gorgeous tiger moth at rest on the green grass perfectly well without having to be told its proper name. Lack of books need not prevent anyone from getting to know the curious caddis worms crawling in their cases at the bottom of a stream, or the butterfly chrysalids that hang on roadside walls, or the wren that creeps in the hedge.

At home Ted and Martin were also finding time to help Jimmy on his new allotment — on the marshland at Southtown under the shadow of a newly erected electricity pylon.

At the age of twelve, in early 1922, he began a series of remarkable diaries — the *Nature Notebooks* — at first making simple jottings about the weather or where he had been, but soon vividly writing in remarkable detail —

bringing his pages to life with observations about the shape of a leaf, or how a bird turns its head. He added, with increasing skill, sketches of fish, birds, beetles and plants, pasted-in maps, press cuttings and photographs. At the end, each book was carefully indexed in his tiny, precise handwriting. Of these he later said:

> They have been invaluable. I jotted down so many things — including meetings with old countrymen who had little market gardens on the edges of the fens. I saw glow-worms, orchids . . . these rich adventures! I spent nights in the woods listening to nightjars and watching long-eared owls come down to feed their young. The magic was there — the sweetbriar along the lanes, the honeysuckle (best at night, of course). And, curiously enough, it was out of that that I first began to write — little things for the parish magazine, occasional notes about things washed up on the beach to the local newspapers.'

Sadly, many of those early notebooks were destroyed in a wartime fire. But they had served a purpose — instilling habits of discipline and daily observation, which he never lost, scribbling down brief reminders as he walked about the countryside, even as an old man. In these teenage diaries he was testing his writing skills as well, occasionally breaking out of the dry, notebook form into half a page of colourful, descriptive prose . . . as if he couldn't resist it! In his *Young Naturalist* column, of 1963, he gave some advice to younger readers that seemed to show him remembering his own methods — and the patience of his pleasure . . .

> If you have kept a nature notebook this year, do make an index for it during the Christmas holidays. You will enjoy doing this, because it involves looking over four exciting seasons and re-living all your outdoor adventures as you pick out the items to be catalogued in alphabetical order.
>
> When you watch a bird pecking about you will want to make a note of what it is eating, and this may mean that you have to go to the trouble of identifying a seed plant or a bush with peculiar berries on it, or some kind of snail or shrimp in a salt marsh pool.

He advised children to use an ordinary exercise book. The result in his own case, was often a yearly notebook an inch thick! Ted Ellis made the study of natural history look effortless — but actually, though self-taught, he had learnt the hard way. Here is a typical page from one of the few remaining diaries — for 1926. He is sixteen years old. The numbers at the beginning of each paragraph relate to his indexing system.

35 Viviparous Lizard: saw one basking on a sunny (Mon. 1st March) bank at Lound this afternoon.

36 Harvest Mice: I caught five in an oat stack (Mon. 1st March) which was being thrashed at Mr Rolfe's, Lound, this afternoon. In my experience a barley stack generally has more mice in than any other, and I have seen fewer in wheat stacks than in oats. Fieldmice are not abundant in stacks, they prefer hedges and fields. A farming man I was speaking to this afternoon said that he frequently came across fieldmice when ploughing, but whether he meant short-tailed field voles or long-tailed I cannot say, though I believe he meant the latter.

37 Harvest Mice As the result of an experiment I have (Thurs. 4th March) found that an average sized harvest mouse weighing 6.48 grammes eats in the course of 24 hrs grain to the total weight of 3.11 grammes. 5 mice ate in 6 days 1000 grains (not weight) of wheat, 1000 grains of barley, and 400 of hemp. They leave the husks, but the grain is of no further use after they have eaten the interior.

38 Flowers (wild) in bloom now around here — Lesser Celandine *(Ranunculus ficaria)*, Marsh Marigold *(Caltha)*, Shepherd's Purse *(Capsella)*, Wood Violet *(Viola odorata)*, Gorse *(Ulex)*, Black Thorn *(Prunus communis)*, Com. Daisy *(Bellis perennis)*, Colt's-foot *(Tussilago farfara)*, Groundsel *(Senecio vulgaris)*, Red Deadnettle *(Lamium purpureum)*, Crocus *(Crocus vernus)* about over, Snowdrop *(Galanthus)* nearly over, Butchers Broom *(Ruscus)* has flowered for about three months past. (Saturday 13th March)

39 Flowers blooming — same as note 38 + Chervil, Stitch Wort *(Stellaria holostea)*, Ground Ivy *(Nepeta)*. (Saturday 20th March)

39(a) Frogs have **done spawning** now. Today I saw the horrid spectacle of a great number of frogs lying crushed and dead all along the edge of a long dyke. I counted 31 but they were not all. Were the culprits boys?

Ted later wrote,

I watched many a harvest being gathered in and in those days there used to be growing excitement on the part of men, boys and dogs in attendance, as the reaper came to cut the last patch of corn in the middle of the field because rabbits and other creatures would be concentrated in this final refuge, and offer great sport at the end.

Much of the corn was stooked and in due course carted, still in ears, to stacks that would be threshed at some time during the winter. In the course of these operations it was usual for many of the smaller animals to be seen darting about as they were disturbed and, here again, boys with sticks and dogs gave chase. There was further onslaught when the day for threshing arrived, the targets being chiefly rats and, in some areas, little red harvest mice.

I also remember that kestrels commonly attended all of these scenes with lively interest, even dashing in boldly to snatch a mouse within yards of the onlookers.

But these were still schooldays. Ted had left Guernsey 'top of the island' with a scholarship to Queen Elizabeth College. But Yarmouth did not recognise the award, and, incredibly, would not waive the red tape which made him too old, by just one day, to resit his exams. Jimmy could not afford to pay private fees. So Ted, gifted even by grammar school standards, only ever went to 'elementary' school. 'I do not bear a grudge,' he said years later. But neither did he ever forget the bureaucratic farce.

So Ted started at Stradbroke Road Senior School, where the children called him Froggy because he was fluent in French. But the 'foreign' boy soon made new friends, and had reason to be thankful for the enforced choice of school. He found the headmaster, Mr Horace Colebrook, sympathetic to his nature studies and his gift for writing. Ted was encouraged, and kept at school until he was fifteen. In one school competition, however — for the best nature notebook — the local press reported that Ted was 'disqualified'! It was thought unfair to let him take part, and a special prize had to be created for young Edward Ellis, as he was 'too advanced to compete with the other scholars'.

A steady and confident gaze from Ted (aged thirteen), posed *(bottom left)* with classmates at Stradbroke Road school

25

Even a folk song learnt in the classroom could set his naturalist's mind pondering. The day they were taught *By Killarney's Lakes and Fells,* a mystery was created for Ted. He could not forget the line 'bright-hued berries daff the snow'. He wanted to know what the berries were! The song didn't say. It wasn't until 1963 that Ted finally visited Ireland on a holiday — but he remembered, and made a trip to solve that forty-year-old puzzle, finding...

There were thousands of holly trees massed in valleys near the famous lakes.

Ted gained consistently good marks in his school work. But his later fluent ability to quote Latin did not come from the classroom — it grew out of its usefulness to him and he taught himself. For, unlike the English names for plants and animals, the Latin system classifies and relates one species to another systematically, providing an in-built memory aid to scientists. It is also, of course, the international language of his profession — a tool which saved embarrassment on at least one occasion. A large party of foreign visitors were touring the northern broads in later years — in fact, two boat-loads of them. Ted called in a colleague to help guide them round. His colleague began, with great enthusiasm, talking about 'willowherb', 'bitterns' and 'waterboatmen' . . . and, though the visitors spoke English, they were baffled by the unfamiliar names. Ted was able to save the day by not only supplying the Latin names, but also using the continental pronun-ciation with which his guests were familiar.

Out of class, in his schooldays, Ted took just enough time off from nature to pursue one other consuming passion; he was an enthusiastic choirboy in the large, traditional all-male choir of St Andrew's parish church, Gorleston. He joined in May 1923 and left only when he moved from the town in 1938. Though his feelings about religion were to go through changes in those years, he always counted the experience of being a chorister as a key influence on his writing . . .

I used to listen to that beautiful script, the Authorised Version of the Bible — the language of the time of Shakespeare, which is the zenith, really, of English. It bit into me.

He relished the oratory of the spoken Lessons, and the sense of rhythm in their prose. And was hearing it, as a choirboy, twice — often three times — on a Sunday, rarely missing a service . . . though he often arrived late with gumboots under his cassock!

In the days of my youthful tadpole hunting on the Bradwell Marshes, near Yarmouth, one of the greatest joys was to peer into the weedy depths of the main dyke and to see there a sort of make-believe shadow world which might be inhabited by almost anything, judging by the number of strange creatures one could fish out of it. The landscape of this underwater country was dominated by enormous aloe-like plants which lay on the bottom in winter and rose to the surface for a spell in early summer; their brittle crimson-brown leaves were the habitation of snails and leeches innumerable, and they seemed forever to be launching little buds which grew into new plants.

And the boy knew well that, by day, much of nature sleeps . . .

I would sometimes walk or cycle to favourite haunts in the country at night, especially in early summer when glow-worms were shining, owls feeding young could be located by their cries and there was the enchantment of watching the shadowy flight and listening to the purring of nightjars at close quarters in a pinewood clearing.

On these expeditions I used to derive pleasure from the scents of various plants such as honeysuckle and sweet briar along the way and I soon discovered that white campions gave forth a carnation-like fragrance at night, as did the more delicate flowers of ragged robin on a glow-worm spangled patch of fen.

Nobody doubted his first love, and the vicar, the Reverend Daniel Dick, encouraged Ted to write nature articles for the parish magazine.

Then his school-days came to an end. Jobs were scarce and any involving natural history were virtually unheard of. So, with a mixture of resignation and amusement, Ted found himself in the unlikely occupation of a sculptor of false teeth. In place of days passed gazing down his microscope, he now spent them bent over plaster models, shaping the originals from which new sets of teeth would be cast.

The factory was owned by Mr and Mrs Price, from Liverpool. Mrs Price had been a member of the Hallé Choir; she was as chirpy as a bird, and often broke into excerpts from *The Messiah* as she went about the factory supervising the girls. I worked in a separate room. In a room next to mine a lad was employed breaking up silica blocks day after day. Poor Don! He must have met with an early death from intake of dust.

It was a curious trade, as well as an unhealthy one. But, in fact, Ted was good at it. Quick to learn and energetic, he was offered training as a manager. At that point, had fate not intervened, his gifts might have dwindled into a spare-time hobby. But Ted, like 'poor Don', developed a cough and, with a history of tuberculosis in the family, it was realised the conditions would ruin his fragile health.

So, in 1925 Ted left the factory, with no prospects, and took any odd jobs he could find, mostly gardening. But he waited patiently for fate to take its course. Ted always had faith that life will come to the aid of people who do not fit into the usual moulds. . . . if they let it. Many years later, for example, Bobby Hanna was the fiancé of Ted's youngest daughter, Suzie and, as he was a jobless, long-haired musician, approached with much apprehension the first meeting with his prospective father-in-law. But instead of the expected frostiness, he recalls Ted saying: 'You are an adventurer, like me. Don't worry — your life will sort itself out.' In 1925, it seems, Ted believed in his own future.

He was growing up in a changing world, but it was still an unusual, and bold, remark when the young, virtually unemployed man told a friend he thought natural history 'owed him a living'. It was regarded as an eccentric hobby for country vicars and gentlemen. For this was still a world in which — at Ceiley's herbalist in Church Plain, Yarmouth — a jar of pickled tape-worms was displayed to advertise a patent cure. The same jars had stood there — Ted's mother told him — since at least 1870.

There were stranger cures to be had out of town. In his talks with country people, he found whooping cough sufferers advised to eat fried mice. (Alternatively, the mouse could be placed on the chest like a brown-paper plaster.) In the neighbourhood of Yarmouth, a dried flounder was clapped on the chest and left there for several weeks while it blackened and shrank. At Burgh Castle, if you suffered from a chest complaint, a live frog might be placed on your tongue, facing inwards so that it jumped down your throat.

And at his great aunt's house in Yarmouth, grisly relics of other bygone country practices remained in an antiques collection . . .

> The place had a fair sized garden, with a tall wall round it and propped up against this wall were several (I think about eight) mantraps with chains attached. No two were exactly alike; some had jagged teeth, and others plain bars of iron for jaws, but all were fashioned like the gin-traps used very widely, until a few years ago, for catching rabbits, rats, hawks, owls, stoats, and other creatures classed as vermin by gamekeepers. The mantraps shown to me were merely antiques, collectors' pieces, but I learnt later that these barbarous contraptions were in common use as a defence against poachers on many East Anglian estates until quite late in the nineteenth century.

Throughout his teenage years Ted's confidence grew and he enjoyed the support of a widening circle of encouraging friends. One, especially, came quickly to recognise his talent. In the early 1920s, at Yarmouth, lived an ageing man who was a famous adventurer. A lifelong naturalist, public speaker and cartoonist, he had once earned his living by exhibiting the carcase of a dead whale in fairgrounds. Now — under the tongue-in-cheek pseudonym of John Knowlittle — he wrote knowledgeable natural history articles in the local press, adding his own illustrations. His real name was Arthur Patterson. He was a Methodist lay-preacher, then in his mid-sixties,

Opposite: Ted was a familiar figure as he explored shore, field or marsh, always with his famous fishing creel

and spent much of his time aboard a strange custom-built houseboat, *Moorhen II,* which was copiously equipped with pickling jars for specimens, pens, writing paper, and all his favourite literature. Breydon Water was his adopted paradise.

On 3 February 1923, Ted and younger brother Martin made an excursion to meet the famous man. They found him welcoming and expansive. Patterson took to Ted quickly and later wrote 'Young Ellis hath the eyes of a falcon and the optimism of a Sancho Panza!' He was mourning the recent death of his naturalist son, Gerald, and Ted came as a consolation. But the friendship was to remain strong until his death in 1935. It began with encouragement to the boy to keep up his nature diaries. 'Observation is futile without keeping a diary' was Patterson's maxim . . . and his own, by then, stretched back over forty years. He also suggested that Ted should read a biography of the great Scottish naturalist Thomas Edward, written by Samuel Smiles. Ted did and found the book an inspiration.

Probably no-one influenced Ted Ellis more than this man — directly through his knowledge of wildlife and birds, but less directly through his hospitality, his faith and his wry humour. (Arthur Patterson wrote comic pieces in the *Yarmouth Mercury* under the title 'Melinda Twaddle's Notions.) It was a maxim of the older man that 'a true naturalist should always be ready to share his pleasures with others.' And if communication was Patterson's gospel, it was Ted's gift. They walked the shores of Breydon together in all weathers, season after season. One of Ted's descriptions of a day in 1926 is preserved:

> I walked along the shore of Breydon from Yarmouth to Burgh Castle. The day was clear and sunny, with little wind and the tide was rising, gradually spreading over the mudflats and precipitating restless movements of wading birds, especially dunlins; thousands, bunched in twisting and turning flocks, flashed like swirling snowflakes at one moment and darkly receded from view a moment later as they rose and dived at speed, whistling as they passed.
>
> A few curlew were also on the move, strong-winged and making the loudest and most strikingly tuneful contribution to the wild music of the estuary. I spotted a raft of about a hundred coot at one point on the main channel and, as is their traditional habit, a few cormorants were perched on the guide posts, some holding out their wings as though to dry them in the sunshine.
>
> When a flock of lapwings came from higher ground to settle on the grazing marshes, rooks and jackdaws rose to mix with them, quickly breaking up their flight formation and creating a great deal of noise as though the newcomers were unwelcome, whereupon the lapwings departed in the direction from which they had come while the black corvids settled again. As the lapwings passed close to where I was standing, they were packed so closely that at times it seemed that their wings touched, producing sharp clapping sounds like those made at times by wood pigeons in courtship flight.

As the waters rose, numerous gulls could be seen moving about over the flats in search of incoming flotsam, while the waders moved away to rest and return when the tide fell away again, laying bare their hunting grounds among the mud-worms and crustaceans.

Arthur Patterson encouraged Ted to meet, and learn from, many old 'characters' of Norfolk — punt gunners, wherrymen and farm workers who had a practical knowledge of nature woven with more humour and less Latin . . . men like Whiley the Gull-Slayer, who lived in a poor little place down towards the South Denes . . .

> I found him in a bad mood and received the impression that the persecution of gulls had done nothing to sweeten his outlook on the world or on people. It is on record that he made a bit on the side through his speciality, by shooting and selling any of the rarer species of gulls which happened to turn up in the neighbourhood.
>
> There was also Little John Thomas, whose wife kept a pork butcher's shop in the town. It became well-known to a few of his close acquaintances that he used to smuggle a good many gulls into the establishment to provide sausage meat, disguised with plenty of sage.

And it was Arthur Patterson who took him to his first meeting of the Norfolk and Norwich Naturalists Society. The day was 26 January 1926, and he took with him a hen pheasant, four live harvest mice and a sponge crab.

In these years, Ted was a prodigious collector — of birds' eggs, shells, bones, mammoths' teeth, feathers, rocks. On one of his early rambles, alone, poking and peering at the ground, he was taken for an 'idiot' and stoned by village children. Ted often recalled the incident, as evidence that an interest in nature had grown in his lifetime from a suspicious oddity into a popular pastime.

At home, he had taken over the garden shed. It was stacked from floor to ceiling with boxes, books, tanks and trays. It was just possible to get a chair in there. But he didn't stop at the shed. 'Ted was a great spreader,' recalls his brother Martin. 'He used to occupy a great deal of space in the house. Once he had filled it up . . . he would move on to another room!' There was once a nasty smell in the house for a while, which Alice eventually traced to a tray of stinking snails under the couch!

Outside, he was growing a variety of plants and bushes. Then he added a 'snailery', which illustrates his youthful studies. It was a little island, part rockery, with several kinds of plant — carrots, nettles, grasses — the whole surrounded by a water-filled moat . . .

> When all was ready for the experiment, I put four common kinds of snail and two kinds of slug there with the idea of finding out something of their feeding habits and of discovering whether all or any of them would escape through the water or remain prisoners.

I soon learnt that garden snails and banded hedge snails were drowned easily when they happened to slip into the water at night, but that one kind of nettle-bed snail *(Arianta arbustorum)* and the large wrinkled black slugs made no trouble at crossing the moat. Some grass snails which had been collected from a sandy cliff slope avoided the water altogether and neither escaped nor lost their lives by drowning. Some of my snails fed on dead vegetable matter and roots; others devoured living leaves of almost every kind, while the grass snails took a fancy to certain kinds of grass.

The large black slugs were noisy feeders; I could hear the rasping sound made by their teeth as they ate green stuff and carrot roots; now that I am older I do not notice the noise made by these slugs.

Ted also discovered that by feeding the common garden snail on certain kinds of leaves he could make it change the colour of the growing part of its shell! And once, having collected some banded hedge snails, he left them overnight in a tin box which had contained sweets. Next day, he found the snails had eaten out all of the lettering on a label inside the tin, leaving the surrounding coloured printing untouched. 'Snail keeping can be full of surprises!' he wrote.

Life was full of surprises for Alice, too. But her reaction when he started bringing home bags of owl pellets was never recorded! That was the time when Ted, in the mid 1920s, joined in a nationwide investigation to discover whether the little owl, which had multiplied since its introduction to England in 1910, was — as gamekeepers feared — a menace to partridge and pheasant chicks. The work involved collecting thousands of the pellets that owls regurgitate, in order to analyse the undigested matter contained in them. The efforts of Ted and many other volunteers eventually saved the species from needless persecution — by showing its diet to be mostly insects, especially beetles and earwigs, together with earthworms. Before the facts became clear, however, Ted saw many grim signs of the gamekeepers' war on the little owl — counting as many as thirty owl carcases hanging on a keeper's fence one day in 1926.

As well as the inhabitants of his snailery, Ted kept other live specimens in a vivarium and an aquarium. Often he treated them with affection, as pets, but he kept them primarily because it 'afforded scope for intimate observation'. Even so, he was far from cold-hearted. There was a viviparous lizard that used to go to bed with him. That lizard, in fact, had many unlizard-like adventures. Caught, after much trouble, in April 1922, 'It travelled in trains and river steamers, and even flew on a kite to a good height,' as well as accompanying Ted on all his excursions until its death in January 1923. And then there was Pete . . .

This is the story of Pete, the missel-thrush. A missel-thrush, in case you don't know, is a large kind of thrush, often called a fulfer, which eats a lot of berries and sings very loudly from the tops of trees and seems to like singing in stormy weather all by itself when other birds are silent.

Pete began a strange adventure when he had not long left his mother's nest. One sunny June day he hopped onto a bed of fine ripe strawberries and became entangled in a net, which the farmer had spread over them. Presently, two boys came along and found him, and one of them took Pete home to look after because the young bird had been hurt by the net. The boy looked in books about birds to find out what sort of things missel-thrushes liked to eat, and every day he collected snails, berries, worms and insects for his new pet.

He had to make a cage and see that Pete had fresh water for drinking and lots of baths. Pete soon got used to his companion and trusted him so well that quite soon the cage was used only as a dog uses a kennel; it was Pete's home but he was free to hop about the garden and fly around. He often followed his friend about the seaside town where he lived and people used to be surprised when they saw the thrush swoop down from the roof-top of a big hotel or from a tree-top and perch on the boy's head or shoulders.

For two years the bird enjoyed life in this way, going out to the cliffs and beach and along country lanes where he picked up the insects and other food for himself. Then one cold, wet winter day Pete caught a chill and died. His friend was broken-hearted and next night went out and gave Pete a sea burial in a cigar box as the tide swept out of the harbour's mouth. He has never known another thrush like Pete.

For a time — in 1925 — Ted also kept racing pigeons, influenced by a neighbour who was a 'fancier', but that interest did not last. More interesting to him was a resident black-headed gull, called Gulliver, which had been shot through one wing . . .

Gulls passing above cause him to give the sky a wistful glance and he stretches his wings as if preparing to fly, then seems to remember he can't, and tucks them to his sides once more.

About the only thing Ted didn't collect for long was butterflies. At the age of twelve, he abandoned the practice, feeling it too costly in delicate lives, and donated his already extensive collection to the Tolhouse Museum in Yarmouth. There it was displayed until it was destroyed — along with many of the other treasures — in wartime bombing.

Ted Ellis, as a young boy and teenager, had — quite simply — the one consuming interest: all his spare time was devoted to natural history. He played no games, followed no sports. Regularly, his day would start with a walk along the beach, passing the pier where he would religiously copy details from the weather gauges: temperature, barometric pressure and wind direction. In the later afternoon, he would return to record them again. But the main purpose was the walk . . .

Whether one takes to the shoreline for a frisk with the dog or is a regular beach-comber, the chances of sea-drift and cliff-tumble, the expectation of a changing scene, the gulls that swing up on the wind, toss of sea, ripple of sand, and wet emblazoning of pebbles into gems, the ragged wing of a storm-victim — even the lonely onion from overboard — provide the novelty that is adventure. The daybreak forager who joins the hooded crows a-scavenging trudges the accustomed span just the same on days that promise no flotsam, for the satisfaction of knowing that he missed no matchwood; this is the fetish engendered in retired sea-dogs, in youths who crave nothing more than 'ducks and drakes' and horseplay . . . and also in naturalists.

What he doesn't record in such writings is that his morning beach-combing was more hazardous than most. In the summer months, to supplement their fixed income, Alice took in lodgers. Then, cramped for space, Martin and Ted would share an upper back room. So to get out in the early hours, Ted had to climb out of the bedroom window, over the roof . . . and down a drainpipe!

A highlight of the young naturalist's year was always his great Boxing Day Adventure with Martin . . .

My brother and I used to plan one expedition into the wider world every Boxing Day. We would study maps of Norfolk and Suffolk and decide upon some new district to visit. Sometimes we set off by train and then walked anything up to twenty miles over the Breckland or along a distant part of the coast. Once or twice we took bicycles a long way by train and covered more country. The main thing was to plan for a completely new experience. This was pure adventure, because we were able to plan everything for ourselves.

Although, when in their teens, the brothers' paths separated, and Martin spent less time following Ted into the countryside, the great Boxing Day Adventure was still kept up and remained a link between them for as long as they both lived at home.

Since leaving the false teeth factory, however, Ted had found no regular work. Months went by and his father, in particular, was anxious. Then in 1926, Ted heard the early broadcaster/naturalist A. Bonnet-Laird on the radio programme *In the Open Air*. Ted was moved to write to him with a vivid description of glow-worms on a fen, and his prose brought an enthusiastic response. Ted was invited to London, lunched with Bonnet-Laird, and was told that if he could first prove his mettle by learning typing and shorthand the BBC would give him work and training in journalism. It seemed the break that Ted had waited for. Back home, Jimmy bought Ted a typewriter (in fact, two! — with an eye for a bargain, he had, typically, found an identical pair at a reduced price) and Ted got to work. Very soon, he was able to type a letter to Bonnet-Laird saying he was ready. Weeks went by but he received no reply. Ted wrote twice but, incredibly, there was still nothing.

Arthur Patterson, meanwhile, had recommended him for a short-term temporary job at Gerard Gurney's respected zoo and aviary at Keswick Hall, near Norwich. Mr Gurney was in a tight spot; his keeper had left at short notice so, on Patterson's advice, he sent a telegram to Ted offering six months' work immediately. Puzzled and disappointed by Bonnet-Laird's silence, Ted accepted and moved into Keswick Hall on 4 October 1926.

Only then did the reply from the BBC arrive urging Ted, of course, to come to London and take up the offer. By a bitter twist of fate, the broadcaster had been ill and Ted's letters had not been forwarded to him. But loyalty was a strong principle with Ted and he stayed at Keswick . . . giving up an opportunity which might have made him one of the first broadcasters in his field and could have launched him years earlier into journalism . . . though it would, perhaps, have left him with much less time for fieldwork. In any case, as he said later: 'I felt bound to honour my pledge.'

Ted remembered the disappointment all his life — even speaking of it on his deathbed — but he never doubted the principle which had influenced his decision.

3 ❧ Old Father William and other friends

ow, at Keswick Hall, began a colourful period which Ted often looked back on with pleasure and amusement, and which was the inspiration for the first notes that he wrote towards his autobiography:

I entrained for Norwich with my essential possessions and was met at the station by a dog-cart by the aged Keswick coachman, William Jessup. On arrival, I was introduced to my quarters — a single room next to the coachman's cottage, opening directly into a yard opposite a cow-house.

My duties were explained to me that I would be taking my meals in the servants' hall — a substantial breakfast, elevenses (bread and cheese and cocoa), lunch and supper. Having brought a spirit lamp, I was able to make myself a cup of tea on rising early of a morning, and the cowman allowed me to take enough milk from a little red-poll cow in the stable opposite.

The hall staff comprised a jovial and well-fed butler, a smart young foot-man, a somewhat irascible Scottish cook, parlour maid, two house maids, kitchen maid (not often seen), and a companion for Mrs Gurney, Gerald's mother, relict of John Henry Gurney Jnr, the well-known Norfolk ornithologist. The Hall, built early in the nineteenth century, was set in a spacious garden and parkland, with adjacent woods and coverts. The aviaries housed a remarkable collection of birds from many parts of the world, some tropical species having to be kept in heated quarters.

A few were free-ranging, tame little ducks and a fierce adjutant stork which demanded lumps of horsemeat at feeding time.

Because some of the birds were carnivorous, Ted was presented each morning with a grisly supply of dead rats and rabbits by the gamekeeper, Mr Vincent, to chop and feed to his charges. The vultures vomited on him, nervously, and the jackasses . . .

When I give our pair of laughing jackasses their daily dish of chopped rat, they drop, alight on the ground, dig their big bills into the dish and flit to the perch with a bit which they thwack upon the branch before swallowing. They greet me with terrific laughter, and do the same when let out into the outdoor enclosure and when shut indoors at evening. Oh! The solemn way they roll their eyes when in the throes of excited uproariousness! I *must* laugh, too.

Then they look — curious, inquisitive. But I interest them a mere fleeting moment after which they go on giggling as if to say: 'Surely you don't imagine you know how to laugh?'

Ted was delighted by everything he saw. He was taken on for six months, but eventually stayed for nine — adding to his many teachers Vincent the game-keeper, Jessup the coachman . . . and Gerard Gurney. In spare moments Gerard allowed Ted to study the papers left by his ornithologist father — correspondence, for example, with Gatke, a pioneer student of European bird migration. J. H. Gurney had, in his time, been Norfolk's leading authority on birds. Writing in 1947 Ted recalled:

William Jessup told me that in his boyhood days a century ago he often witnessed the rescue of cattle at Holkham Mere. There were right and wrong ways of pulling out a beast: the right way was to back a wagon as close as possible to the floundering animal and to pass the haulage tackle over the vehicle; a direct pull at a low angle was almost certain to injure the unfortunate beast.

Another time, William told him that any juniper tree found in a Norwich village was, in his youth, treasured; as a groom he had followed the custom of giving a sprig to ailing horses, finding that moderate amounts brought glossiness to their coats. From Mr Vincent he learned that not all white stoats are in winter dress; the gamekeeper had tracked as many in summer and thought some might be albinistic. He taught Ted that stoats were great travellers, for though he shot about forty a year their numbers were always replenished.

Ted also got on well with the birds and animals in the collection — making friends of them all, and enjoying their capers . . .

One of my favourites was an Indian adjutant stork, a huge grey bird with an almost bald head and a neck pouch which he could inflate rather like a sausage-shaped balloon. He roamed freely about the gardens, sometimes standing like a statue by a lily pond and sometimes flapping his great wings and running after people. He had an evil way of snapping his beak and a fierce glint of mischief in his grey eyes. If I tossed him half a pound of horse meat, he would catch it in the air and swallow it at one gulp and rush at me for a second helping.

Adjutants live as saucy scavengers in many Indian towns, where they are held in respect and because of their usefulness are not molested, so they have no fear of people. Old Father William, as the Keswick stork was called, was jealous of an African porcupine which lived in an open pen in the gardens. He would stand watching the porcupine for half an hour at a time hoping to make a peck when the animal was not looking, but never getting a proper chance.

Then one day, just after I had given the porcupine a nice turnip, William leaned over the railings and tweaked the hair on his enemy's head. The porcupine rushed backwards at the stork's face, every quill bristling. William only just escaped and, looking greatly shocked, he walked over to a garden seat and sulked. I never saw him try to torment the porcupine again.

Ted never grew tired of watching the animals . . .

Our pet porcupine has a low hut filled with straw, and a small hole where he can squeeze his way out into his enclosure. I call 'Hello!' and he trots out from strawland to grunt for an expected turnip, swede, mangel or morsel of bread, or to enjoy his chin being scratched. Here is a bit of his reasoning — on three or four occasions I've noticed it: it is his wont to eat turnips in his hut, but he has to fetch them from the yard and take them through the little hole. Now and then I give him an extra-plump vegetable too bulky to pass in the entrance hole. So Porcy, on discovering it is vain to try pushing it in, calmly crunches the peel off and tries again. Then, if it is still too big, eats some. Anyhow, as soon as it has been diminished sufficiently he carts it in with delight.

There was more to looking after the creatures than he could have expected. In the early weeks, he had to go armed with a dustbin lid to feed the porcupines in case they fired quills at him.

Gerard Gurney bought birds from ships arriving at the docks. At the end of these sales, there would be a huddle of dismal creatures that had not travelled well — dull-eyed, drooping birds with their feathers dropping out. These forlorn remnants would attract Mr Gurney's pity and he would buy up anything still breathing. If they survived the journey back to Keswick Hall, Ted would be presented with these limp invalids; he had many a sleepless night trying to restore lustre to an exotic plumage, and put the sparkle back in lost and troubled eyes. One was a yellow crested Cassique . . .

We have just one, a poor sickly fellow, though his plumes are bright — black and gayest yellow. The trouble is his nasal system, and he cannot draw the pure air through his nostrils, for they are constantly blocked, so he's unhappy and has to gasp, splutteringly, through his pale-bluey beak. He is intelligent and somewhat mischievous. Anything in my hand I happen to pass his cage with, he begs for and is really disconsolate till satisfied. If it is elderberries I give him a few — he eats them. If it is chopped-up liver, well, his eagerness goes off as soon as he possesses this coveted morsel and he leaves it on the sandy cage floor and *asks for more*. Poor little rascal! He 'potters and pingles' over biscuit meal and crumbled hard-boiled egg, covets grapes a little, and strives hard to master the swallowing of sticky banana; but his breathing and feeding get muddled, so he doesn't actually obtain enough food to sustain life and is gradually starving.

Sadly, the Cassique eventually died.

Even if he had no sick patients, Ted still had to stir himself at two o'clock in the morning, for the constant warmth required by the tropical specimens meant that the boiler had to be stoked in the small hours. And then there were daily earth-worms to be found and dug up. Somehow, though, he found time to cycle into the city in the evenings, and attend botany classes at Norwich Technical School. He also found time to explore the woods, and look for smaller life . . .

Though I have spent many an evening out late studying slugs, snails, woodlice, millipedes and other small creatures of the night by torchlight, in woods and marshes, on heaths, dunes, pastures and arable land, it has only once been my fortune to discover the shell-tipped carnivorous type of slug abroad in the darkness. This was in the kitchen garden of Keswick Hall, when I watched one of these lithe, fast-moving molluscs in the act of devouring an earthworm newly captured as it peeped from its hole.

Under the bark of a rotten elm log on another ramble at Keswick, a beetle squeaked at him! It was a black *Cychrus caraboides* nearly an inch long . . .

The squeaks were wheezy and alternately loud and soft, and when I held the insect between my fingers, I saw that the sound issued from the rapidly pulsating abdomen and appeared to be produced by the expulsion of air, rather than by any special stridulating organs such as are used by some other beetles (and grasshoppers).

In January 1927, one of his birds hit the national newspaper headlines — in an incident that had more to do with farce than real drama. As Ted later recalled:

One day the local hunt came by (the Dunston Harriers, I think) and this so startled our largest 'bull' rhea that he jumped over the park rails and crouched under a nearby cedar tree. Shortly afterwards, I enticed him back into the enclosure with a promise of biscuits and that was the end of the incident so far as the bird was concerned. For the greater part of the following week, however, newspapers all over Britain were carrying stories about a giant bird, described variously as an ostrich, emu or cassowary, said to have escaped from a Norfolk zoo. There were tales of it terrifying the inhabitants of villages round about and evading every means of capture until finally it was reported as having been taken by surprise in the parish of Mulbarton.

The incident bred into him a lifelong scepticism about alarmist newspaper stories. As for the bird . . .

Early in March he began to boom like a bittern and he spent most of May and June incubating not less than seventeen eggs laid in a common nest by two wives, after which he became a proud father guarding his brood.

There, next month, Ted left him — along with the South American ostriches, Sarus cranes, near-extinct New Caledonian kagus, the buff-backed heron, bishop finch, alpine choughs, and many other friends. His time at Keswick Hall had come to an end. Writing in 1933, he said:

Passing on the torch of his experience — Arthur Patterson dictating *Wildfowlers and Poachers* to Ted at Ibis Lodge

Aviculturalists at the time vied with one another in seeking possession of rarities and were thus a threat to their survival in various parts of the world. For instance, we had a pair of the beautiful grey kagus, with ruby eyes suited to their habit of night prowling in search of worms in their home far away in New Caledonia . . . Looking back, one realises that such birds on the borderland of extinction should not have been imported for the pleasure of hobbyists and sightseers, although there was also a serious side to the business pertaining to the scientific study of bird behaviour. I remember that the eggs of the South American San Blas jay were unknown to science until some were laid by our pair in captivity.

In March 1926 Arthur Patterson had retired from his job as a school attendance officer and moved to Hellesdon. There, in his free time, Ted had continued to visit him. In February 1927, however, after the death of his wife Alice, the old man came back to Yarmouth and, when Ted's employment ended in July, the two were again able to spend more time together around the familiar haunts. For the next year they continued their rambles. Ted began attending botany evening classes at Yarmouth Science School — and earned a little money as a part-time laboratory assistant there as well. He also put a notice in his window at Gorleston — TYPING WANTED — and was visited by an elderly man scarcely recognisable without face-paint, though known to millions. It was Ted who typed the memoirs of the original 'Coco the Clown', who had retired to the seaside town.

In the daytime, he was usually free to roam the countryside. Though Ted was still only eighteen, Arthur Patterson was impressed by his ability to name every plant or butterfly they saw. Ted visited him aboard the house-boat nicknamed *Pickle-tub* and at his home, Ibis Lodge, on Saturday nights for a 'mardle'. 'Ted is my spaniel,' the old man would tell friends, jokingly. Ted later wrote of his mentor:

> I was fortunate enough to enjoy the companionship of Arthur Patterson in the last thirteen years of his life, on long walks in the country around Yarmouth, on his beloved Breydon Water and the Broads, and in the intimacy of his study as he scribbled articles, books and lively pen-and-ink sketches or was joined on a winter's evening by a coterie of naturalist friends. Sometimes, I accompanied him when he gave talks, illustrated by humorous lightning sketches, in village halls and schools, and as he threaded the streets of Yarmouth or Norwich, calling on numerous acquaintances, among them the old Breydoners who figured in his published reminiscences.
>
> We would call at Yarmouth fishing-wharf on the chance of collecting rare specimens saved for his inspection, or stroll down to a beach where draw-netters were hauling in their catch. His sprightliness and sense of the comical ensured a welcome wherever we went. There was the salt of the sea in the mellow timbre of his voice, which echoed the dialectical blend special to his native town. He looked about like a Sir Thomas Browne, seeking new wonders and delving into mysteries with the eagerness of a child of the Renaissance.

It was during this year that Patterson made the third attempt to write his memoirs — calling the book *Wildfowlers and Poachers*. The experience, he wrote, made him feel like 'a gentle curlew bidding kind goodnight'. And it was Ted who sat beside him, night after night, typing it — discussing it, sentence by sentence, in the bond of true friendship. The book was published in 1929.

Arthur Patterson was not his only teacher, however; these were years of many influences . . .

> From the 1920s onwards, I somehow or other met such a lot of the leaders of botany, the great men, the sort you met at the British Association. This was purely because I was doing the sort of things they were organising.

Yarmouth, and north Norfolk, were unusually rich in amateur, but intelligent and respected, naturalists. Also in the county were the families and friends of many professionals whose interest had taken them to posts far away. Ted met many of them, taking every opportunity to broaden his circle of teachers and friends. His walks on Gorleston beach, for example, were often taken with Chester Doughty, one of whose hobbies was to collect bird feathers scientifically . . .

> In this way I learned to recognise feathers from various parts of a number of different birds. His samples were stuck in rows on sheets of stiff paper. They comprised a full series of primary and secondary pinions from one wing, half of the tail, some wing coverts, tail coverts and plumes from the shoulders, back, flanks, breast and a series of axillaries from underneath the wings.
>
> Bodies washed ashore provided much of this material and from time to time additions to the collection came from a variety of birds found dead on roads and in other places where they happened to come to grief. Many years later, my old friend Chester Doughty's feather collection found a permanent home in Norwich Castle Museum.

Chester also collected moths, butterflies and other insects. These teachers came from all walks of life — with little in common but their enthusiasm. Chester, for example, a former Oxford cox, had trained as a barrister but, having independent means, never practised.

From 1922 Ted also knew H. J. Howard, a teacher, who was keenly interested in slime moulds — mycetozoa. He encouraged Ted to collect them . . . impressing on him that it is worthwhile taking the trouble to attain scientific skill and to seek a close acquaintance with life forms other than the obvious kinds like birds, butterflies and flowers.

Dr Sydney Long at Norfolk and Norwich Hospital became another friend and took Ted birdwatching at weekends on Scolt Head Island. Dr Long was the founder of the Norfolk Naturalists Trust, the first society of its kind in Britain.

Yet another quite different man was Philip E. Rumbelow, by trade a master plumber but a gifted self-taught naturalist and archaeologist who kept immaculate leather-bound nature notebooks written in beautiful copper-plate script. He and Ted went on excursions, often accompanied by Harry Hurrell, manager of the newspaper offices in Yarmouth and a skilled microscopist who encouraged Ted and Martin's interest in the instrument. 'He used to show us different things under the microscope . . . moving things,' Martin recalls. 'What better way to fire our interest?' Under the microscope, Ted found there are wonders . . . even in a heap of dust!

> A good many people go through life without ever looking down a microscope, just as they miss seeing the stars through an astronomer's great telescope. It

Ted found colourful stories, deep knowledge and a countryman's humour as he talked to Tom Brooks *(top left),* and enthusiasts like Fred Cook, pictured *(top right)* with Arthur Patterson

In old age, Philip Rumbelow, naturalist and archaeologist, was still a fine teacher

seems a pity not to make use of these wonderful aids to sight, if only to satisfy curiosity.

For instance, what seems duller than dust, as it lies on a shelf or coats the bonnet of a motor car? Look at a few samples of it under a microscope and what is it then? There will be mineral grit, soot and ash, of course, and very often a variety of small hairs and vegetable fibres, webs and fluff.

In addition to this rubbish, and depending on where and when the dust was collected, there may be pretty iridescent scales from wings of moths and other insects, starry scales from the surfaces of leaves, boat-shaped skeletons of tiny dried-up pond plants called diatoms and many kinds of pollen grains from the stamens of flowers. There is also a lot of living dust, both animal and vegetable.

Put a little dust into some water which has been boiled and cooled; after a few days, swarms of microscopic creatures hatched from the dust will be swimming in the water. Spores of ferns, mosses, liverworts and countless fungi journey through the air as dust; many of them have peculiar shapes and they are often ornamented with knobs and spines. Being so much lighter than seeds, they can be wafted to great heights and carried all over the world by air currents.

Then there was Dr Hugh Ramage, who gave him demonstrations — as vivid as firework shows — of the spectroscopic analysis of metallic elements in plant tissue, as he 'scanned the flames produced from carefully weighed, dried samples, reading off the various light bands which revealed the presence of a wide range of elements'. It fascinated Ted, who was just beginning to study fungi, to learn in this way that mushrooms absorb and concentrate rare metals from the soil. 'Dr Ramage even followed this up by extracting beads of pure silver from mushrooms for the fun of the thing.'

The list of his teacher-friends is endless. There was Alice Geldart, a botanist and long-serving member of the Norfolk and Norwich Naturalists Society, Mr D. Drummond, Manager of Boots chemists, and Ben Dye, a former bird taxidermist who had become blind but by touch alone could still identify any bird specimen handed to him! There was Claud Morley, a well-known entomologist and expert on certain groups of insects, who lived in a moated grange in Suffolk; Miss E. L. Turner, the ornithologist and pioneer bird photographer; Arthur Mayfield of Mendlesham, Suffolk; Tom Petch of North Wooton, the authority on fungus-attacking insects . . . who once received a unique birthday present from Ted — a specimen of a beautiful spider fungus completely unknown to science for him to study.

From one friend he learnt to spot flint scrapers left by stone-age people on ploughed fields. 'Another collected snails and beetles and mounted them beautifully in his cabinets at home. Still another took a deep, scientific interest in dragonflies, and more than two or three used to dab treacle on trees to attract moths at night.'

Amanita pantherina photographed by Ted in 1976

Further afield, Ted was befriended by W. B. Grove, of Birmingham, a maths teacher and venerable student of rust fungi who had — among other books — published in 1884 the first comprehensive description of bacteria and yeasts in this country. Ted described him as one of 'my special mentors'. They corresponded for many years and visited each other. The older man impressed on Ted the incompleteness of laboratory work and the importance of also studying organisms in their natural environment.

Countless countrymen added to his knowledge, too — men like Mr Osbourne of Lound Run, who was often mentioned in the diaries. Ted knew wildfowlers, including the famous Jim Vincent, head-keeper on Whiteslea Estate. One countryman, Tom Brooks of Belton, may stand as an example of the help he gained from many. Tom kept fowls, bees and grew vegetables on three-and-a-half acres at Belton Fen. He was a wheelwright and carpenter, a friend of Arthur Patterson. Ted wrote, on 10 August 1925:

> I first met Mr Brooks of Belton this evening when I was commissioned by Mr Patterson to fetch some natterjack toads. I thought him a very kindly man. He took great pains to find me the toads. He showed me his flowers, which he cultivates to sell away, and his birds. He keeps an Egyptian goose which was shot in the neck some three years ago on the marshes towards Reedham, and which he had put in his 'hospital' as he called it, an enclosure, along with two

male Mallards. In another enclosure he keeps two teal, some wigeon and a pintail drake — they all looked very happy (in spite of the fact that they were on the moult) in confinement amid natural surroundings.

That evening, Ted stayed late. Tom talked to him of woodpeckers, kingfishers, bats and mice. Over tea in his little hut, he told him stories of the past, and showed him his collection of stuffed birds — sending him home not only with the toads but with a number of interesting slugs as well! After this Ted was to visit Mr Brooks many times over the next few years.

Ted's voice had not been heard in public yet. The occasion came in November 1927 — and his first talk, 'Some Delights of a Young Naturalist', was an immediate success; it inspired a meeting of Yarmouth Rotary Club to set about re-forming the Great Yarmouth Naturalists Society — defunct for more than ten years. Reporting the meeting on 16 November, the *Eastern Daily Press* described him as 'a young man who is developing into an acute natural history observer.' The Society was formed a week later and, by February 1928, had over a hundred members. Ted was its first joint-secretary, sharing the duties with his friend Mr D. Drummond.

These were the days before modern slide projectors. So Ted illustrated his early talks, following Arthur Patterson's example, by drawing and painting his own large, colourful sketches on the backs of huge pieces of wallpaper, and pinning them to the walls around him at lectures. Thus surrounded, he began:

> I should like to speak of the things which keep a naturalist busy and cheerful, of rambles in the woods, of hot June days on Belton Common watching snakes and vipers in the heather, of mild still summer evenings in Fenland stepping across dewy seas of grass sparkling with glow-worm lamps, of observations of our queer local race of toads (the natterjacks), of pond-hunting, insect-grubbing, snail-keeping, or mouse-catching in the harvest fields, of hours on Breydon, sunny Fritton Lake, the Broads, the river nooks, of birdwatching all the year round — sea birds, shore birds, marsh birds, woodland birds; at breeding time and when thousands of migrating flutterers are on the move in spring and autumn.

The speech included a vivid picture of one of his excursions in July 1926 . . .

> I spent a morning out with a shrimper. A chill foggy atmosphere shrouded the dawn as I went to the river side. A few shrimp boats were slowly going towards the harbour mouth and returning again — they were waiting for the mist to clear before putting to sea. Old Bob, with whom I was going out, was of a philosophical turn of mind and did not arrive so early. Being an old hand, he didn't come to waste time hanging about. His son came with us, and we rowed over to his trim shrimp boat. The brown sails were hoisted, the auxiliary motor started, and we swung out with head downstream.

The haze around became fainter, so with a few other craft we crept out of the harbour and went southward to Corton. The ponderous dredges, packed one each side of the boat, were dropped into the sea. As she dragged them we could feel by gripping the ropes how they scudded unevenly over the rippled sandy bottom. I was revelling among the queer animals which he called the 'rubbish' in his catch. I sorted out hundreds after hundreds — pink-marbled suckers (interesting fish having a flat disk underneath by which they fasten themselves to anything, even one's fingers!), cuttles, spangled and spotted, rich purple, pink and gold-lit green, looked at us with fearful eyes from the mass of gorgeous life brought from out our dull sea.

In 1928 Ted was writing regular short articles in the *Eastern Evening News* and *Eastern Daily Press,* often under the pseudonym 'Chirp', on subjects ranging from gulls, bats, hedgerow flowers, the need to keep footpaths open . . . to, in December, one on the afforestation of Breckland . . .

Ploughs, idle for Christmas, lay like sleeping ruffians on the scene of their misdoings . . .

A letter written to his brother at about this time captures his high spirits:

Touch, touch — anything. Feel it, tremble at it. Life awake and bound away — echo — echo — spirit seek out — oh find, oh know, the real, the true, oh lovely life a-rhythming. And Age mundanely dubs him drunk. 'Oh, sartinly.' The above is a specimen of pop-pop English — it needs a certain amount of courage and roguish abandon in the manufacture. It is my reaction to such stuff as 'I remain your humble and obedient servant'. Poof! my beloved greybeards — youth must run and put new flowers in your garden. Damn your yew peacocks and box edges, and window-box geraniums *à la* trimmity. Let me play and joy in my words. Mug them not so immovably. Let our urge go moulding sweet naïve words — pealing bells — let them crash sometimes! Dull block men, fed, soured, livered with that vile poison conservatism — I would plunge you naked into gorse and bramble thickets and drop you cheerfully into bogs. Oh Age, I am unjust. Your cogs are rubbed flat — you cannot kick. Poor Age, so miserably cautious!

Now he was offered another temporary job, to help with the summer exhibition at the Tolhouse Museum, Yarmouth. It proved to be a turning point. He impressed the authorities and his work brought him to the attention of the Norwich Castle Museum where a new, permanent post was about to be created.

4 ❧ The museum years

ed never forgot his first 'home' at Norwich Castle Museum . . . a desk shoved into the old condemned cell!

The new post was advertised in August 1928. But his friend Henry Howard had worked there as education officer since before 1922, giving daily lessons to schoolchildren, and had passed on glowing reports of Ted. Tolhouse Museum recommended him too, and so — it is believed — did Gerard Gurney who was an influential figure in the area. The Castle's curator sent Ted a copy of the advertisement, when it appeared in the specialist press, to ensure he applied. Nonetheless, the appointment of an unqualified teenager to a professional post was remarkable then and virtually unthinkable now. Ted took with him to that interview nothing but a stack of his own *Nature Notebooks*. Yet these — each page a testament to his observation and enthusiasm — were evidence to support his claim: 'Life has been my university.'

The new job reinforced the friendship with Henry Howard . . . and also with Reggie Gaze, Henry's inseparable companion . . .

> The two friends shared interests in wildlife photography and in the study of many delicate and beautiful little fungus-allies known as myxomycetes or mycetozoa which they discovered in great wealth in the undergrowth of woods and hedges in the county. Reggie Gaze's happy hunting grounds were chiefly in Costessey Park, then an unspoiled paradise full of nightingales in summer and abounding in trees, flowers and butterflies. Following in the tradition of that pioneer of bird photography, Richard Kearton, Howard and Gaze developed outstanding skills in recording the domestic life of birds at the nest. Moreover, both were always extremely careful not to intrude so as to cause the desertion of nests by the owners.

Ted's new job was, officially, 'Natural History Assistant'; it would be many years before he was graded as a full 'Keeper'. But, in a department of one, that didn't stop him being responsible for geology, zoology and botany, all the natural history collections, and for answering any questions in these fields from the public. He welcomed the fact that the job gave him practice and experience over a range of subjects which, nowadays, are tackled by a department of four specialists. 'Apprenticed' to the last of the Edwardian and late Victorian amateurs, Ted had their tradition in his blood. But now he represented a new breed — a professional working in a fast-changing service.

They were exciting times; throughout the country, large museums were shucking off an old skin and struggling to find the purpose and the sharper focus which distinguish the museums of today. Ted's generation inherited museums which housed wide-ranging collections from around the world, a legacy of Victorian tastes often lacking coherence and — at worst — little more than a collection of curiosities. The new demand was for more limited but more detailed, more local but more structured displays. The changing attitude suited Ted, and he found himself in the vanguard. Why 'amaze' visitors with the head of a gargantuan beast they will never meet — when you can teach them to find amazement in the nearest hedgerow? Throughout his life, Ted was a champion of East Anglia's importance to natural history, and in this new job he was encouraged.

His natural curiosity was a gift to the department. Throughout the 1930s, in his own time, Ted carried out countless small, acute studies of tiny facets of Norfolk's wildlife . . . each following his principle that 'to study nature in the round, there is no better exercise than taking up a general study of a single species of plant or animal from every possible angle'.

He took his own advice repeatedly. When, for example, he set up a small display case of spire shells, he had a wealth of information at his finger-tips. For his own interest, he was carrying out a study of the distribution and ecology of three kinds of small spire shells living in brackish and fresh waters of East Anglia. One of them had the odd ability, unique among British snails, to reproduce with just one parent. This self-contained creature, *Potamopyrgus jenkinsi,* also lived with equal ease in salt- or freshwater. Though known in Norfolk's coastal waters, so far it had only been found at one inland, freshwater site. Ted's studies indicated that we could expect to see more of it soon, as its parthenogenetic reproduction (from an unfertilised ovum) makes it a ready pioneer . . . 'any stray individual finding its way into a new area can found a colony straight away.' That proved to be true, and the snail was soon common.

In the museum of the early 1930s, Ted had to be a jack-of-all-trades . . . collecting specimens, hanging pictures, helping to prepare bird skins. There were few staff, beyond a carpenter and uniformed attendants. Ever ready to 'fill a gap', he even donated a tooth (which had to come out anyway). To this day, it is part of the dentition of the Castle's human skeleton!

There was also another, more controversial, occasion when Ted went 'beyond the call of duty'. The carpenter came to Ted one day and said: 'I don't know what we're going to do, Mr Ellis. That picture of Nelson that we lent out — well, it's come back with a hole in it! I daren't tell the curator. Will you have a look at it?' Ted did more than look. Seeing that the hand had been damaged . . . he repainted it! His artistry was skilled enough to go unnoticed. Years later, he owned up, and pointed out his handiwork to a visiting art expert whose reaction was more one of horror than of praise!

In another of his special studies, Ted encouraged a contractor employed on dredging work to send him specimens of the plants that were brought up. Typically, with his love of dialect, he did not neglect to record the local names by which the workmen knew them . . .

In those days the now rare water soldier was familiar enough to be known generally as 'pickerel-weed' and I found that several marsh grasses and sedges went by the name of 'cheat' or 'chate' which meant simply that they were classed as small-stuff (compared with proper reed and thatching sedge) in the relation that 'chat' potatoes bear to larger ones.

We have some remarkable local names for plants in Norfolk, not found elsewhere in Britain. The guelder-rose is called 'gatter-bush' or 'gattridge' and sometimes the 'Whitsuntide-flower'. Tussock sedges are called 'nat-hills' and the sand sedge is 'net-rein' here and nowhere else so far as I have been able to discover. At Hickling they call the black bog-rush 'star' which is its Scandinavian name, presumably introduced by early settlers from over the sea. Coarse blanket-weed is known on the Broads as 'raw', but I have not come across this name for it away from that district. Terms such as 'bunks' and 'bunds' are applied to several different wayside plants in different parts of Norfolk. It is not long since I learned that ragwort is called 'gauntlet' or 'gant-weed' in some parts of Norfolk and I would not be surprised if there are still many old local plant names which have not yet been listed with their botanical equivalents.

Not long after he started at the museum Ted was offered a short working holiday that deeply influenced him — a fortnight which he remembered as a highlight of his life. It was spent at the laboratories of the Marine Biological Association in Plymouth where, with a group of other young people, his eyes were opened to the vast field of marine research, and he experienced modern scientific approaches to creatures of the harbour and the shore. He took with him his old microscope and the silk handkerchief that he habitually draped over it to keep dust off. That white 'veil' earned it a nickname, 'the bride', among his fellow-students. It appealed to Ted's sense of humour and, thereafter, visitors to his study were always introduced to 'the bride'. To Ted, more seriously, his microscope was a significant reminder that he was shaped by a long tradition; as he wrote in 1981:

For over fifty years I have been making regular use of a long-barrelled, narrow-staged brass microscope which first saw service in 1870. This instrument has an interesting history. Its solid base was once a candlestick — one of a pair bought from Forder's stall in Yarmouth market place by Christopher Stacey-Watson, who fashioned the microscope to his own design. With remarkable foresight, he made the nose thread of exactly the size which was adopted universally somewhat later, so that it takes modern objective lenses.

Stacey-Watson was a keen local naturalist and published valuable papers on the herring. He lived on Yarmouth's South Quay, being a shipping agent, salt merchant and proprietor of the Yare Fishery Works until his death in 1896. One of his close friends was Harry E. Hurrell, an ardent microscopist who in his spare time studied pond life, notably polyzoa and rotifers, on which he became an expert. Stacey-Watson presented him with the candlestick microscope and he, in turn, gave it to me by way of encouragement for a young naturalist in my teens.

. . . I have since made thousands of drawings of fungus spores with its aid, to an accuracy of half a micro-millimetre, and the discipline of using it over the years has been of inestimable value. It has also continued to serve as a personal link with those fellow-enthusiasts with whom it was associated long ago.

On his return from Plymouth Ted was immediately asked to give a talk to the Yarmouth Naturalists Society. Thinking they must be tired of his face — since he had given several talks — he decided on some mischief. Arranging to be billed as a visitor from Scotland, Ted gave the entire lecture in a heavy Scots accent . . . dressed as an octopus! It fooled no-one. Ted was too familiar a figure to go unrecognised there. Not only was he a frequent speaker, he even delivered notices of meetings on his bicycle!

At home there were changes. His brother Martin, unhappily apprenticed to a tailoring firm after his grammar school days, decided to leave his job and study at home. His parents agreed, but the most active encouragement came from Ted who bought him books and, after Martin successfully matriculated, urged him to go on for a degree. 'There are courses at Norwich — I'll pay your train fare!' He did and, armed with that ticket, Martin went on to gain an external degree.

When Ted went to the museum, several galleries were taken up by glass cases housing the famous Gurney collection of birds of prey. In the reorganisation it was decided to relax these naturalistically mounted exhibits, in order to convert them into case skins — a form in which the specimens can be more readily examined and stored . . .

In the process their glass eyes were removed. I noticed that the commonest eye colour in these predatory birds (eagles, hawks and owls) was some shade of yellow, brown being another common tint of the iris, while in just a few cases a a hawk had ruby eyes or an owl totally black ones.

On this project Ted worked alongside a taxidermist from Liverpool whose face was cherry-red due to constant handling of the arsenic paste that was used as a preservative in his trade. Ted later suffered several weeks of illness now thought to have been due to arsenical poisoning contracted through handling the stuffed birds.

He recorded that — as in humans — the colour of eye does not seem to have any functional significance. And his own eyes remained hawk-like . . . even observing the tiny life-and-death dramas, outside his work-place, of the armadillo woodlouse or pill-bug . . .

> These woodlice move around at night when there is enough moisture in the air for their method of breathing. If they topple onto their backs on flat, hard surfaces, they may not regain a footing and if exposed later to the shrivelling heat of the sun when the night is over, they die. In the days when I worked at Norwich Castle Museum I often found these creatures suffering from this predicament on the steps of the mound, and my efforts at rescuing them were not always in time.

At the museum, now, began the work which stands as his most conspicuous memorial there. In the early 1930s, word came of a new display technique from America. There, the traditional glass cases packed with row upon row of stuffed animals and birds were being replaced by three-dimensional landscaped vistas in which creatures which would naturally occur together were arranged in realistic postures amidst their native setting. The Americans called them dioramas. Both Ted and the curator, Mr Leney, were fired with the idea of showing Norwich city-dwellers some of the wilder scenes in their own county — through the diorama technique. The result was that between 1931 and 1936 Ted supervised the creation of a set of such exhibits then regarded as the best in the world, and still admired today by museum specialists for their painstaking accuracy.

The finished gallery was named 'The Norfolk Room' and, fittingly, in 1987, it was re-named 'The Ted Ellis Norfolk Room'. For, although other specialists — notably the landscape painter Francis Whatley — worked on them, Ted was a guiding force behind them all, designing, collecting the reeds, stones, bushes and other materials, co-ordinating the work, and taking artists to see suitable Broadland scenes for the background paintings. Above all, he set the standard of detailed realism. Real bushes, for example, were used in the 'Norfolk Loke' vista, with their foliage carefully preserved. Ted modelled artificial replicas of the flowers and berries. If reeds were shown in a setting where tidal waters would rise and fall, it mattered to him even that a little band of mud should be shown at their base — where the water level had dropped. The first two dioramas were completed in 1933 and, though there was then a delay due to shortage of funds, two more were completed by 1935.

Meanwhile, in the absence of modern computers, Ted set about the creation of the next best thing, an ambitious card-index system designed to show at a glance — and record — in a readily retrievable form — the occurrence of every species of plant and animal known in Norfolk: where it had been seen, when, how often, and by whom. It was his dream to bring together in this way the experiences and observations of all Norfolk's amateur and professional naturalists, encouraging them to contribute their findings and learn from each other.

Thousands of cards were printed with a simple map of the county on one side so that, in those days before the National Grid system was widely adopted, locations could be precisely indicated. Parts of his card system still exist at the Castle. It was originally housed in a desk presented in 1934 by the Yarmouth Naturalists Society. The presentation was partly in gratitude to Ted — still a driving force behind the Society — and partly in celebration of the centenary of the publication of *A Natural History of Yarmouth* by two young brothers, C. J. and James Paget.

It was a fitting coincidence. For what was new about the Pagets' work, a century before, was that it recorded every living thing found in a single area of Norfolk and that it set these records out alphabetically so that it could be easily consulted — like a 'dictionary of Nature'. Making use of the system of Latin name classifications which had been in existence for less than a hundred years, the Pagets detailed everything within ten miles of Yarmouth market place. Ted's efforts were an update of their work, and an ambitious attempt to extend it to the whole county.

The Pagets were heroes for Ted — as for most Norfolk naturalists. He collected memorabilia, including rare letters, and once copied from the introduction to their book an extract in which James, wryly, says: '. . . as I look back, I am amused in thinking that the mere knowledge gained in the study — the knowledge of the appearances and names and botanical arrangement of plants — none had in my after life any measure of what is called practical utility. The knowledge was useless; the discipline of acquiring it was beyond all price.' James used that discipline to become one of the most eminent surgeons of Victoria's reign.

Although Ted remained a naturalist — and his observations therefore retained 'practical utility' — he, too, was to emphasise the value, in itself, of 'discipline' — be it acquired through microscope work, through regular journalism or through keeping notebooks.

If one other historical figure had to be chosen as having an outstanding influence on Ted, it would be Sir Thomas Browne. The eighteenth-century doctor and amateur naturalist/historian never wrote a book, but poured his enthusiastic observations into letters to scientist friends. In this way, his successes were preserved. Ted — who once spotted a tiny rust fungus on a hedgerow plant as he drove past at 40 miles an hour — clearly pictured Sir Thomas as a similar character, reining in his horse as he rode to visit patients over the Surlingham and Claxton marshes. Sir Thomas, too, was an acute enough observer to notice some of the fungi as he travelled about. In fact, to modern eyes, his statue in Haymarket, Norwich, perhaps gives too grim and pompous an impression of a man who, for two years, kept a bittern in his back garden, and turned both the garden and his house into a colourful collection of curiosities. He made the first records of many of Norfolk's species though — again oddly to the modern mind — often included notes on how best to eat them!

In these years, Ted was still learning from countrymen as well . . .

Whenever there is a scare about the threat of foot-and-mouth disease spreading among our livestock, I recall some of the observations made to me on this subject by Jack Smith, a familiar figure at the old Norwich Cattle Market, who handled large numbers of animals driven there from the lairs near Trowse railway station up to the 1940s. He could neither read nor write, but he had a remarkable memory for figures and could recount the transactions and experiences of his long life most vividly. Outbreaks of the 'murren' were familiar enough to him in his youth and it was formerly looked on as something to be coped with by curative action rather than by wholesale slaughter. Jack told me that beasts which had passed the crisis of their affliction almost invariably sought ivy to munch, as though instinct told them to seek it out as medicine.

Ted had become a popular figure at the Castle and made many friends — men like Tom Wake, who had a lasting influence on him, and Arthur Hunter, now a professor, who recalls a youthful adventure with more than its share of mishaps:
'I first met Ted Ellis at the Norwich Castle Museum in 1931. I had joined the staff there from school as a junior assistant and, although our interests were quite different, we became close friends. In the following year, we decided to have a holiday together on Skye. The original idea was that he would be a pillion passenger on my motor-bike. Unfortunately I found that I was too young to get an insurance for a pillion passenger so I bought a cheap side-car for the bike. This turned out to be the cause of some of our later troubles!

'We set off for Skye with Ted packed in the side-car surrounded by all the baggage and bits and pieces we needed for a two-week holiday. When we stopped on the roadside for eats (or other natural reasons), Ted always vanished into the neighbouring fields to examine the local flora. On occasions, later, this turned out to be irritating when something had to be put right on the machine by me. I remember an amusing incident on the way out when, on such an occasion, the local bobby appeared. He challenged Ted with: "Wot are you doing in yon field?" Ted said: "Botanising!" Reply: "Wot's that?"

'Apart from such events, all went well as far as the Pass of Glencoe. In those days it wasn't the smooth, fast road it now is. It was just a rough track covered with big stones and boulders. I had never seen anything like it and, with the bumping Ted was suffering in the side-car, he was afraid that the spindle would break off and throw him in the road. It took us about ninety minutes to go 14 miles. We did, however, reach Kyle of Lochalsh and crossed to Skye with the ferry to arrive just at nightfall.

'Our intention was to put up as boarders somewhere. However, in our first few miles on the way to Portree we burst a rear tyre. We pushed the bike and side-car to where we put up at a hotel. This was a much more posh affair than our limited finances could afford and it made serious inroads into our cash reserves. The next morning I stuffed the tyre with grass, and we drove slowly to Portree. There we bought another tyre, and also found accommodation at a watermill house with a Mrs McCrae. We decided to take just breakfast and evening meal so that we did not have to return at midday. Ted and I shared a double bed and read each other stories before going to sleep. Ted used to double up with mirth over P. G. Wodehouse.

'On our first trip round Skye our troubles started. The jogging from the rough roads broke the side-car spring. I patched it up with a block of wood which did not add much to the travelling comfort for Ted. The next disaster was to spill honey into the side-car. This all went to the bottom where we couldn't reach it to clear it up! For the rest of the holiday we were followed by swarms of wasps! A few days before leaving Skye for Norwich the rear spindle of the motorcycle broke in two parts. I managed to fix it by putting the spindle back the wrong way round and screwing the broken halves into one cone. This got us as far as Spean Bridge when the cone broke in half! We put up at a local boarding house for the night and found an elderly garage man prepared to make us a new spindle (which would not be possible these days). All these troubles had exhausted our cash. Already we had both wired home for extra money and neither of us cared to do so again. We therefore hoped to reach Norwich in one day.

'Our troubles were not over, however. A front tyre burst and I found a scrap merchant where I bought another tyre for half-a-crown. Then the driving chain broke and I wasted time trying to rivet it up with a stone (as I had no hammer in the tool-kit). This failed and then we found that there was a garage just over the hill where we could get a clip to repair the chain.

'With all this, our money was now at a very low ebb and we could not reach Norwich that day after all. We put up at a miner's cottage just outside Stirling. There we were in a double bed in the kitchen. A big wall clock kept us awake all night. We left early in the morning with just enough money for petrol and a bar of chocolate each for a twelve-hour journey. When we got back I threw the side-car away and never used it again!'

Back at the museum, another colleague introduced Ted to a quite different world . . . making friends of *Drosophila* — the small flies best known to the layman for hanging around pantries or home-brewed beer and wine buckets, but of much interest to geneticists on account of the large size of their chromosomes . . .

> Romantically, as I now see it, I was first introduced to the then budding scientific importance of *Drosophila* by Michael White in the 1930s when he spent a few months working with me in reorganising natural history displays. He showed me how to collect the tiny fruit flies in jam jars with ripe banana, in the museum's central courtyard.

In 1937 Michael White wrote the first English text book on chromosomes and in time became one of the world's leading geneticists.

Meeting the public and encouraging people to take an interest in Nature was an active concern of Ted's. By the mid-1930s, there was a mounting unemployment crisis — far exceeding official statistics since women could not register, and neither could men who had not worked. Ted decided to turn his natural history to service by, at least, alleviating boredom and to this end ran classes for the jobless.

Meanwhile, his own special studies continued. One of them had his brother scanning the skies from Gorleston beach almost as if an invasion were expected. It was! For Ted had joined in a nationally-organised investigation to chart movements of migrant moths, butterflies, dragonflies and hoverflies. He enlisted volunteers — including his brother — to stand for hours counting the arrivals over the sea. Not satisfied with that, he arranged for crews on lightships to send him reports of flying insect swarms, and also of migrant birds, from stations off the coast between The Wash and the Isle of Wight . . .

> By this means we were able to gather information about movements . . . besides learning of insect swarms swept out to sea involuntarily by air currents from time to time.

This evidence of massive numbers of insects bound on some inland journey often becoming unwilling 'passengers' on strong winds and thermals was one of the main discoveries of the investigation. But Nature also provides, for the observant, a different kind of easily-read daily record of butterfly movements.

> I made a special point of visiting the buddleias in certain public gardens to count the numbers of each kind of butterfly on the same bushes day-by-day. If there were scores of red admirals one day and only one or two the next, this suggested that the flocks might have moved to another district.

Clearly, he found buddleia-watching a fascinating pastime!

Pioneers of a quiet revolution — Ted and other staff
at the museum in about 1933

All this time Ted was still living at Gorleston, making a one-hour train journey each way. Since the train got in only four minutes before he was due to start work, and left again soon after he finished he was becoming a familiar figure . . . *running* to and from the station! With his lifelong casual and practical attitude to dress, he became well known for nonchalantly crossing the city in folded newspaper hats on rainy days!

Those train journeys were forging an important friendship which would eventually lead him into journalism . . .

> I was introduced to Tom Copeman by A. H. Patterson . . . at the offices of the *Eastern Daily Press* in London Street, Norwich in the late 1920s, when he edited the *Eastern Evening News,* and was encouraged by him to contribute notes to his 'East Anglian Miscellany'. Later, when (from 1928 to 1938) I used to travel by train from Yarmouth to Norwich Castle Museum daily, we often found ourselves companions when he joined the train at Reedham, where he lived for part of this time. In 1932 he agreed to my introducing the feature 'Norfolk and Suffolk Wildlife' as a supplement to the East Anglian Miscellany.

This was an ambitious project, close to Ted's heart, and it complemented his work at the Castle. 'Norfolk and Suffolk Wildlife' eventually ran from 1932 to 1938, with many writers, under Ted's supervision, contributing articles and descriptions of species to be found in East Anglia. Each year he wrote an annual index and, as time went on, he wrote more and more of the articles. From the early 1930s, he was also contributing occasional letters and general nature articles to the local press under pen-names like Peggotty or Pedlar. His style was well-developed, as this piece from the *Eastern Evening News* of 17 May 1930 shows . . .

> The shrews that mystify us with their shrill chirruping among the grass tussocks when we go into the fields and lanes are nest-making somewhere among the dead, mossy roots of old tree stumps. It is possible to sit on a warm bank now and, if you remain very still and noiseless, to see one enter a hole with a sere oak-leaf in his mouth, while he sings happily about his business. In meadows, too, voles are dancing about in sunshine and have snuggeries of fine, dry grass. When you disturb their gambols, they rush into hiding like lizards.

Such pieces, and his regular wildlife series, were completely unpaid work — but they gave him journalistic experience, and were to lead to paid work later.

> After Tom Copeman became editor of the *EDP* in 1937 I continued to contribute notes of various kinds to the *EEN* under Harold B. Jaffa's and Alfred Cope's editorships, including items for 'Over the Tea-table' and 'Moldwarp's Gardening Notes' (begun during the Second World War). In 1945, Tom Copeman invited me to contribute articles on natural history topics for the *EDP,* and I wrote a few of these over the pseudonym Natterjack.

> Then, in 1946, he suggested that I might write a short 'In the Country' feature daily for the editorial page and I undertook to do this . . . I remember that Tom was a keen reader of 'A Country Diary' in *The Guardian* when I used to see him on the train from Reedham and this may have persuaded him to introduce something similar into his newspaper when the way was open.

Ted's job put him in touch with naturalists outside Norfolk — academics at Cambridge, for example — and he was soon developing a reputation as a Sherlock Holmes of nature, consulted by doctors and hospitals over poisonings and mysterious deaths. A child's stomach was sent to him after the mother said she had given the two-year-old bottled blackcurrants. He discovered that, tragically, the hard skin and pips from the fruit had choked the child. In another case, he was able to trace the unexplained death of a five-year-old to poisonous berries. Authorities in many counties consulted Ted over poisonous fungi, and antidotes for poisonous plants.

His questioners sometimes came from even further away. His description of one visitor in 1931 illustrates his early concern with natural or biological alternatives to chemical pesticides . . .

> The Government entomologist of Fiji, Dr H. W. Simmonds, called on me to solicit help in finding a stock of certain bluebottle-sized flies *(Mesembrina meridiana)* remarkable for the predacious habits of their maggots, which feed on other maggots in cow dung. He explained that in Fiji because the climate was specially favourable houseflies bred freely in dung on the pastures and had become very troublesome on the islands. He hoped that by introducing *Mesembrina* the pests might be brought under effective control biologically. I happened to know that the required ally was to be found plentifully from May to October on some grazing meadows at Surlingham and a stock was secured without much difficulty.

The flies were taken to their new home, and Ted heard no more until, in 1962, he met another visitor from Fiji who, incredibly, proved to be Dr Simmonds' next-door-neighbour . . .

> I was delighted to hear from him that the introduction of *Mesembrina* had resulted in the complete banishment of houseflies in one of the Fiji islands and that there was now no fly problem at all. Not only was vast expense and trouble saved thereby, but a solution was found before the advent of DDT or the more recently discovered insecticides. The biological control of pests has often been found completely successful in various parts of the world, but we in Britain tend to prefer spraying and dusting the countryside with an ever-increasing range of death-dealing chemicals which only too often kill both friend and foe.

Apart from his more obvious work creating and rearranging displays, and as a consultant, Ted made an invisible contribution to the museum. Collectors who have, in some cases, devoted a lifetime to their passion take seriously the question of where to bequeath the fruits of this long labour. Often, the desire to leave it in safe hands makes them look mostly at the reputation of the individual staff. So Ted, simply by his presence, attracted donations and bequests to the Castle.

A famous example, it is said, was Margaret Fountaine, daughter of a rector of South Acre, who travelled the world collecting butterflies and left her collection, along with her sealed journals, to the Castle. After her death in 1940 the journals remained untouched, as a condition of the bequest, until April 1978, when they were edited into a popular book — *Love Among the Butterflies*. It is said her choice of the Castle was influenced by meeting Ted once at the beginning of his career. She was, by then, in old age and Ted asked her how she had survived her years in the jungle so unscathed. She replied that her secret was to take regular baths with an infusion of creosote! Ted told the *EDP* writer and author Jonathan Mardle that 'she was small and swarthy — looking as if the creosote had soaked in!'

The public came to the museum, too. They brought Ted questions. They also brought tins, boxes and strange packages. There were exotic insects and spiders, lizards, snakes and other reptiles found lurking in imported bunches of bananas. Once there was a locust found amongst cauliflowers delivered to the Norfolk and Norwich Hospital. A solitary black widow spider brought to him, and left overnight, became a mother by morning — and emergency measures had to be taken to deal with dozens of babies! Even more deadly was the strange object sent to him by a Yarmouth man . . .

> When, some years before the last war, a 14lb lump of waxy material trawled from the North Sea was sent to me for identification, I at once thought it might be spermaceti. One of my great-grandfathers was an old sea-dog and it was from his tales, through my mother, that I first heard about the spermaceti and above all, the miraculous ambergris produced by the sperm whale. As I had been told as a child that ambergris was something washed up on the beaches and very precious, the fact added excitement to all my beachcombing especially when, as happened occasionally, I came upon a lump of paraffin wax at the tide line! On one occasion, my treasure trove proved to be spermaceti, similarly white, waxy and translucent; but the more greyish, marbled, strongly odorous ambergris never appeared.

So Ted thought he could recognise the mysterious substance that arrived on his desk . . .

> But, knocking a piece from it, pounding it up with pestle and mortar and heating a sample in a test tube demonstrated that the substance was not of animal origin. Mystified, I sent a piece to the geology department of the British Museum. It turned out to be TNT which, as any explosives expert would say, is a highly temperamental substance always to be treated with respect!

Young people came to the department and received their first encouragement from Ted — including many who are now professors or heads of large departments at universities and at museums in this country and abroad. Indeed, two of the four specialists now employed at Norwich Castle Museum — John Goldsmith and Bob Driscoll — both knew Ted in their schooldays.

Many budding naturalists came my way, reporting their discoveries and seeking a little help with their studies. One of them who took a particular interest in wayside plants seen as he cycled from Wroxham to school in the city went on to become Britain's foremost authority on the intricate digestive processes taking place in cows' stomachs.

One day, in 1933, a typical older visitor was standing in front of a case of shells, looking puzzled but interested. He was a short, brisk man clutching a handful of his own shells which he was trying to match with the display. Ted went over to help, got into conversation, and found the man was a retired soldier, Captain Maurice Cockle, now living on a remote fen near Surlingham. Captain Cockle, an ex-India Army man, had gathered the shells from his own dykes and waterways. Ted was, of course, fascinated and before many minutes the hospitable old man had invited him back for a first look at Wheatfen. It was a turning point in Ted's life. For, unbeknown to the Captain, his land — from a scientific point of view — proved to be 150 acres of the richest, most diverse fenland habitat in East Anglia. It was a naturalists' paradise and, though neither of them could have suspected at the time, it was Ted Ellis's future home!

It had twice the flora of the famous Wicken Fen; it was rich in bird life; it had Montagu's harriers breeding here, bitterns and — whilst the flowers were marvellous, of course — there was woodland going down into wet woodland, or carr, then the fens and a whole chain of little waterways, relict peat diggings of medieval times.

So I set about mapping it, mapping the flora and publishing an account of where all these plants were living, beginning an introduction to some of the other things, and then encouraging friends to come here.

As early as 1935 Ted put the British Association for the Advancement of Science into gumboots and conducted them round Wheatfen during their stay in Norwich. They seem to have been a volatile crowd at their evening meeting, as Ted recalls:

Professors Poulton and MacBride almost came to fisticuffs on the stage of the Assembly House when debating alternative theories of evolution.

The visitors brought a profound change to the lives of Captain Cockle and his wife, as well. Soon their home was a Mecca for specialist observers.

Caught up in Ted's enthusiasm, Captain Cockle walked around proclaiming: 'I never knew these things existed!' and was soon looking around for himself, bringing things to show Ted as he worked on a pamphlet — *The Natural History of Wheatfen*. He welcomed all the visitors, telling them 'Come over any time!' And Ted seized on the Captain's systematic nature, and his taste for filing systems, by enlisting him to begin recording and indexing everything found alive at Wheatfen . . . from mites to birds.

Though no naturalist, Captain Cockle was curious and enjoyed experimenting. He kept goats. He had planted two trial rows of daffodils to see if they would flourish on the marshes. The daffodils didn't prove the commercial success he hoped for but Ted was able to celebrate their fiftieth anniversary in due course — and they were still healthy in 1987. The Captain also contributed another lasting feature to the scene — a tree-top observation post rising by a series of three strong, wooden ladders to successive platforms wedged in the branches of a stout tree. It looks perfectly at home there, providing a panoramic view over the Broads, but, in fact, it comes from a very different world. It is modelled on a *machan,* an Indian tiger-hunting platform. Though it has been repaired and replaced several times, its original form has been preserved.

At the Castle Ted had tried to expand the Pagets' comprehensive recording to the whole of Norfolk. Now, in a sense, he did the opposite — turning his attention to a mere 150 acres and spending the rest of his life making new discoveries there, proving that the more closely you look at something small — even the piece of ground between your feet — the more there is to see. He said at the end of his life he had hardly begun on this task, yet he involved many other people in it, and Wheatfen has become the best-recorded fen in Britain. It has been described by David Bellamy as in the World Heritage class — as important in its way as Mount Everest — because of the early, detailed recording of its changing life . . . a task which is still continuing.

Ted's first account, on the distribution of the plants, was published in 1935, and the more comprehensive *Natural History of Wheatfen* in 1939. Another publication on microfungi and their hosts followed in 1940. Among his many helpers, A. E. Ellis (no relation) carried out research on the woodlice and harvestmen that occurred there.

A new chapter was beginning for Ted and, at that point, an old chapter closed. On 31 October 1935 he attended the funeral of Arthur Patterson. Ted left on the grave a simple spray of wild flowers gathered that morning from the banks of Breydon.

By the mid 1930s a young Yarmouth schoolteacher, Phyllis Chambers, was sometimes among the friends with Ted at Wheatfen. She was to become his wife, and their story actually began many years before. As children they had known each other, slightly, in Gorleston. Later, her father, Jack — a keen sailor — had a bungalow at St Olave's where Arthur Patterson kept his houseboat. 'I knew Ted in our early days when I was a child, but I was four years younger than him. He was a well-known sight on Yarmouth beach and in the country — with the fishing creel that he always carried to put specimens in.' But then Phyllis had gone away to Goldsmiths' College to train as a teacher, returning only for holidays.

'I don't say I met him then — but everyone knew him. He was just a character — always with boundless energy. I think I first talked to him in 1932, when we met on a marsh. I was botanising for my teaching diploma; I did a project on the weeds of the cliffs, ponds and marshes of St Olave's. There was, at that time, a very rare plant which is no longer rare, the marsh sowthistle. In those days it was thought to be extinct but had just been rediscovered on St Olave's marsh — only two or three specimens. He saw me looking at it and regarded me with grave suspicion, fearing that I might be going to pick it or dig it up!'

Phyllis qualified and came back to Yarmouth in 1933, to live with her parents Ada and Jack. She was interested in natural history — but not exclusively. She was involved in amateur theatre and was an accomplished piano player but had turned down the chance to take a degree in music in favour of teaching. She and Ted met again when he was sent — virtually under orders — to learn to dance! In those years, Yarmouth and Gorleston were like villages in the winter months when the summer visitors had gone; everyone knew everyone. So she immediately recognised him one night in the unlikely venue of the local dance hall.

'He just turned up . . . and sat there!' Phyllis recalls. 'His mother had thought it was time he went out more and learned to dance.' Gradually, he did learn — the waltz, the Boston two-step . . . 'The Gay Gordons was a great favourite with Ted. But he could thoroughly disrupt a Scottish reel without even thinking about it! We used to have to get one each side of him and drag him through *The Dashing White Sergeant.*'

At one of those dances Ted offered to buy her a drink and Phyllis, amused by the young man who 'had a reputation for being rather a rigid character', wryly ordered a gin and lime — something only a notorious woman would drink. She thought he would be shocked but Ted was not worldly wise in such matters — so gin and lime she got!

They were engaged in 1937.

'When we were courting, he invented a character called Uncle Snarlet, who turned up in a lot of the letters he wrote to me.' One such letter began:

Snarlet, I must explain, is my peculiar uncle. He is always turning up, as a substitute for expectations and disappointments alike. If I am rid of him for a whole day it is because he is hatching some scheme for the night, and vice versa. His hobby is adding checks to his history in as many colours as he can pick up. His dignified countenance masks a terrible ingenuity of thought and his consequential behaviour disguises a purposefulness only equalled by the basking crocodile . . .

Soon, the letters were elaborated with Ted's imaginative and idiosyncratic story-telling . . .

UNCLE SNARLET DRINKS TURNIP WINE

I met the old boy this afternoon: he always seems to turn up like a seraph if not an angel when you are hid away from me. 'M'lad, don't fret,' he says, 'Think of some pretty thing for her.' And I reply in the smallest whisper (quite inaudible even to the tell-tale LITTLE BIRD) — 'Oh, Uncle, but you *don't know!*' and leave it at that . . .

It appears that a month or so ago Uncle had an ache inside; the kind of ache that comes to a hermit once in his life and is responsible for all the vacated hermitages one finds at every 'old-world' spot. Snarlet felt suddenly like a chick in an egg or a butterfly in a chrysalis (you will understand one or the other). Without more ado (it was lark time) he cleaned his teeth with brick-dust, put ice in his bath, shaved with the favourite hacksaw, broke his daily mirror, put bedsocks in pocket, set a match to the hermitage, telephoned the fire brigade for a false alarm elsewhere, and from the crane on the quay sprang aboard the first out-bound cargo boat. This done, he lay still.

Next day he awoke, panged. Hailing a stoker in his best blend of Hottentot dialects, he received a superior look-over and dropped all subterfuge, only to find English and innnnnnumerabbbble other tongues failed where Russian achieved audience with the Kaptan. This latter was a sort of Soviet Amazon, and yet a woman: she broke his head, then nursed it — duty, then pleasure, first the fist and then the fingers. Snarlet forgave.

After a wonderful trip (during which Uncle counted 316 porpoises — by a coincidence just the number of days to pass before our wedding, dear!), the ship put in at a tiny port in Sweden, for contraband. Uncle spotted the country, though at night, by a shipment of barrels labelled 'Turnip'. He had never seen these common vegetables so conveyed before, and remarked on the rumminess thereof to a wharf man whose face loomed at the mouth of a pipe quite a yard long. This man was dumbfounded, so of course Uncle heard nothing from him.

Presently they hove anchor, the wind got up so that the vessel rocked and a cask of 'Turnip' gurgled. This was enough to confirm anyone's suspicions. Snarlet's brandy-flask was soon gurgling empty and gurgling full again, with . . . t- - -p: sh! sh! sh! Was it Vodka?

In half an hour Snarlet was in charge of the ship: the other people were in fear of their lives. He followed a tramp (this being the extent of his navigational foresight) and by sheer chance came into Yarmouth. Approaching the crane, he deserted and was in lodgings shortly with a final hiccough. He repeated to himself many times 'A port in Sweden, a port in Sweden, a port in Sweden'.

Then he remembered it was no longer necessary to go all that way. Was there not a Mr Wilsdon?

He dreamed — colour honey-gold . . . bouquet more overpowering than valerian on cats . . . flavour as distinct as can be from salt-waves rolling round the palate . . . altogether stunning.

> If to Sweden you manage to run up
> Be sure that you ask for the tunnup.
> They'll Rushyer to Yarmouth
> Because of yer sourmouth,
> But with gunup you'll still be the oneup!

With tunnup it's fun up till doneup, come sunup there's noneup, did you call 'Boo', dear?

Ted and Phyllis were married on 8 October 1938, at Gorleston parish church — to the accompaniment not of the traditional Wedding March, but *The Dance of the Sugar Plum Fairy*. 'Well', says Phyllis . . . 'It was Ted's favourite tune!' The wedding was a simple affair, Phyllis in a blue frock and Ted sporting a new suit which he continued to wear for years afterwards. There was no expensive honeymoon as they had only just managed to scrape together a home — largely of second-hand furniture and gifts. But they had a happy time roaming the countryside and one day went gathering blackberries, along the River Tas, to make wine . . .

Miraculously, the blackberries must have been contaminated by a wild 'champagne' yeast for the wine resulting from the effort proved to have a clear and sparkling quality which we have never achieved since.

The Ellises' first home was at the corner of Martineau Lane, Norwich. 'In those days,' says Phyllis, 'it was country. You looked out of your back door and there was a meadow. We had a quarter of an acre of garden and we bought gorse bushes, rosemary bushes, sweetbriar roses and some tamarisk bushes which we planted all the way round the edge. We planted the piece of grass in front with that beautiful South American crimson clover . . . much to our neighbours' horror. It wasn't a lawn in the accepted sense!'

Then, in 1939, the war broke out.

5 ❧ The war years

he war cast a shadow over many lives — not least that of the Ellises. During its course they were made homeless, but before that there was a grim prediction of early death hanging over the naturalist.

Early in 1940 Ted, inspired by his adventurous half-brother, applied to join the Royal Navy. Instead of following in Percy's footsteps, however, he was told that he probably had, at best, only five years left to live. An X-ray taken during the medical examination showed that his lungs had been ravaged by tuberculosis — so badly that, effectively, little more than one of them was functional. It explained years of breathlessness which had crept upon him so slowly as to be almost unnoticed, and it confirmed that the slight cough he had developed in the false tooth factory was a sign of the disease they feared. Ted had every reason to know the full, ugly picture of tuberculosis, for his own father's health was gradually being ruined by it — reducing him, by slow degrees, to a white-faced wheezing figure, bad tempered through constant pain. So the Navy turned Ted away, shaken, with advice from the doctors to 'take things easy'.

Ted's 'cushy' war was, in later years, to earn him the resentment of some other naturalists of his generation, who sometimes felt he had been able to stay at home and develop his career while they lost five years. In fact, it seems that Ted — who genuinely admired Percy's career and was patriotic — was bitterly disappointed to be turned down by the services.

Rather than follow the doctors' advice he now threw himself into the only service open to him: he became an air-raid first aid volunteer for one or two nights of the week, and also took fire-watch duty on another, sitting on the windy Castle roof with a field telephone. As he climbed the long, steep stairs to the roof he wondered, no doubt, how long he would be fit enough.

As yet, there were no bombs. The first months of the war brought only first aid lessons at the ARP's Surrey Street headquarters in the old chapel, and extra work at the Castle, covering for the missing men. Yet the City was not quiet . . .

I made a curious discovery in passing through Norwich during the blackout. The prevailing hush of traffic revealed a great population of house-crickets in both old and new parts of the city. From Mile Cross boundary down to Fye Bridge, under the shadow of the Castle, all along Ber Street and City Road out to Old Lakenham wherever the chirp of one cricket left off, another began. The effect was puzzling for people in the streets; several stopped to listen, quite keyed up; they had never heard the crickets before . . . owls have been extending their beats citywards; I have heard them upsetting urban dogs and no doubt some of the sparrow roosts have been a little depleted. 'Tu-woos' and other cries are heard in places where they are unfamiliar; I woke up myself to the wailing of a tawny owl, sounding at 3 a.m. curiously like the echo of an air-raid siren . . .

Village children, awakened by late squabbling in a nearby rookery, cry 'What's in the dark, daddy?' They will not be alone in these little terrors now that the country is invading the town.

At the Castle, the naturalist turned his knowledge to the needs of the war effort in a series of 'dig for victory' displays, showing people how to get the most out of allotments, and how to grow their own food. He made a 'hero' of the plentiful potato with an exhibition of spuds (every imaginable type) collecting a line of specimens stretching right round the museum's top gallery, backed up with a barrage of information — the history of the potato, its diseases, where it came from — and a bombardment of recipes: pies, scones. . . even bread could be made from potato! Never doing anything by halves, he wrote a poem celebrating the virtues of 'Dr Potato', and another parodying a popular radio show — 'The Brains Trust Considers The Potato':

The introduction's past, and now
McCulloch makes his formal bow.
He clears his throat and glances round,
Quelling some little ribald sound.

Before your fancies take to flight
I'll warn the question isn't light:
A child of six (await the thud)
Politely asks you 'What's a spud?'

Campbell's first: he's met them often
And sampled some that wouldn't soften
When in the Andes he made trek
And with the Redskins shared a break.

His belief is, they came from Eire
And grow best, like the Shamrock, there.
As for the name, an Implement
Its Victory blessing must have lent.

Huxley is quick to make it clear
That wild potatoes don't grow here
Or in the Emerald Isle; their rise
Was under South American skies.

67

Joad is horrified that Plato
Never knew about potato.
The guests, Sir William first, are sure
We ought to eat earth-apples more.

Miss Lee in duty bound must add
That 'soggie' taties make her sad:
Women should know it is their cooking
To which Lord Woolton's chiefly looking.

The question-master has his quip
He wants the skins to have a zip:
And beaming gratitude, he wishes
That all may get more chips with fishes.

Another display took advantage of a topical interest by illustrating camouflage in nature. All the pattern, mimicry and evolutionary subterfuge practised by birds, fish, insects and mammals were shown. The lessons humans learn from them were exemplified by a model of factories imitating the imitators, and painted with camouflage patterns.

In 1939 Phyllis's mother, Ada, had been stricken with cancer and, after an unsuccessful operation in February 1940, came to spend her last months with them at Long John Hill. She died on 17 June that year — the day France fell, and Broadland cruisers crossed the Channel along with a small Armada of yachts, tugs — even rowing boats — to rescue British soldiers waiting, sometimes standing up to their chests in the sea, at Dunkirk.

At home, Phyllis was running the local MAGNA (Mutual Aid Good Neighbours Scheme) in Lakenham . . . and seems to have paused just long enough to have their first baby, John Augustine Ellis, who was born on 2 April 1941. She was soon back at work, leaving Alice, Ted's mother, to take charge of the baby. The Ellises had also organised a rabbit and poultry club and were surprised to find a hundred people at their first meeting!

There had been a whole year of 'peace', during which they heard only one or two practice sirens. During that time, Anderson shelters were issued to any homes with a garden. Ted and Phyllis had one big enough to take two small wooden bunks, dug down into the earth and covered over with soil. They built a sandbag blast-wall around the entrance ramp, and hung a thick curtain across the doorway . . .

Even the dug-outs we have been making in our back yards this autumn have had their quota of wild inhabitants. During the period of excavation in one pit of regulation size, no less than fifteen frogs and toads and one newt arrived in a night and tucked themselves into sand-trickle snuggeries at the corners. By day, a queen wasp, a humble-bee and a drone-fly were seen probing for winter hiding places in the sides; two funny grubs of ermine moths, a couple of grass-hoppers and some tiny insects called springtails tumbled in at odd times, together with several long black devil's coach-horse beetles prowling with their upturned tails after dark.

The shelters were damp, draughty and uninviting and tragically, many a handyman was tempted to fix wooden doors rather than curtains across the entrance, not realising they would shatter into hideous, lacerating 'shrapnel' in a blast, the splinters maiming families who would otherwise have been unhurt. Ted was on one of the first ambulances to go out, in Norwich, to such a scene. That night a woman lost her legs. Similar disasters on other nights left grim memories for the volunteer first aider.

When the peaceful months ended, the Ellises were right in the thick of it. 'The planes woke us up,' Phyllis recalls. 'Then we heard a bomb whistling down and landing in the pig-sties on the other side of Martineau Lane, next to Lakenham Baths.' The warning siren did not sound until afterwards. It was one of the first night bombs to hit the outskirts of Norwich and Ted, shocked and unthinking, got up and went outside the back door to look. As he did so a blast, so close that they never heard it, shook the house, smashing windows and splitting walls, tearing doors off and sending the electric stove flying across the room to jam the door closed behind him. Ted, somehow

Typical of Ted's energy and attention to detail is this wartime display on allotments

69

still standing, found himself groping round the outside of his home . . . to step in through a front door that was lying sideways. Phyllis was climbing to her feet in the choking dust. Pieces of flying metal were embedded in the kitchen dresser. They found the baby, in his carrycot, silent and still, completely blackened by soot and sparkling like a Christmas tree under a fine covering of powdered glass.

For a long moment they looked at John — then he opened his blue eyes through the soot. He was unhurt and, at seven o'clock that morning they were dancing on their lawn, cheering and laughing . . . congratulating each other on being alive! For more than luck lay behind their escape; it also owed something to a strange insight. Ted always believed he was psychic and, in later years, the night of the bombing would be one example he often gave. There had been a row that evening. He had insisted they sleep in the Anderson shelter instead of the upstairs bedroom. He couldn't say why . . . it was just a feeling. But the shelter was damp and, with a new baby, Phyllis wasn't giving in to vague 'feelings'. Eventually they compromised, curling up downstairs under a heavy oak table, and wedging the baby's carrycot under the piano, against the chimney breast. In the blast, the upstairs ceilings were blown down and, says Phyllis, 'The baby, at least, would have been killed.'

The Ellises didn't move out. They were offered council accommodation but, as they owned their house, decided to stay. For six months, they put up with temporary brown paper ceilings, tarred paper windows, and walls with cracks big enough to put your hand into.

Phyllis now became used to carrying knitting whenever she went out with the pram — to pass the time if she had to duck into the nearest air-raid shelter. Ted, on first aid duty, was under nerve-racking orders to head for the ARP headquarters, come what may, as soon as the sirens sounded. One afternoon, he was strafed by a German aircraft's machine-guns as he was spotted, all too visible, running through the city. He made a dive and, unhurt, popped his head up a moment later to appreciate a macabre joke: he was sprawled behind a gravestone!

The unglamorous horrors of night bombing started an exodus from the city. Even families who still had homes began leaving at night, a long column trundling push-chairs, carrying blankets and old sleeping bags. Literally hundreds preferred to sleep in the safety of the corner of a field, or under a hedge bank. Phyllis, as local MAGNA representative, would find homeless families queueing at the village hall in pyjamas and dressing gowns. On one occasion, she promptly organised the opening of a local school as an emergency centre. An official reprimanded her, later, for setting it up 'without proper accounts'. 'I told him where to put his red tape,' she recalled.

They moved out of their home in September, whilst repairs were made, then returned and just had time to get straight before — in June 1942 — it was hit and gutted by incendiary bombs. This time the loss was almost total — clothes, furniture, irreplaceable papers and specimens, and family heirlooms, an old Bible Box inscribed 'Elys' which, though the family Bible it once contained was missing, had been handed down for generations in Ted's family. As volunteers fought, ineffectively, to control the flames, Ted was seen calmly picking his way through the chaos carrying out . . . a jam jar full of water beetles!

A whole stick of incendiary bombs had hit the roof of the house. In keeping with Government advice they had had a bath full of water ready but when that was gone water had to be brought in buckets, from a nearby pond. Official fire-parties were ordered to stay in reserve, in case of more serious fire in the city, so little could be done. 'If it had not been for the fine help of soldiers and neighbours, who eventually had six stirrup pumps going, I think the whole row of houses might well have gone,' Ted wrote in a letter to Philip Rumbelow. Little was left of the Ellises' home but the outside walls. Ted and Phyllis had never set much store by possessions but, in later years, the simplicity of their surroundings did owe something to the memory of that night . . . the blackened remains were a stark reminder that anything can be taken away, at any time, without warning. Though they had not been wealthy, their home had contained some fine linen and pieces of walnut furniture handmade by Phyllis's grandfather. Of the furniture, only one scorched desk could be rescued. Providentially, however, Ted had packed many of his notebooks, specimens and his old microscope in a seaman's chest which was in the garden.

Now the young family was homeless. They lodged, at first, in Lakenham Hall (now demolished), where thirty soldiers were billeted in a stately music room with an army cook who was a former chef from a top London hotel. He seemed able to conjure delicious meals out of the air and, as the soldiers were not rationed, the Ellises at least ate well. Then, for three months, they lived in lodgings at Rockland St Mary — on a hill just half a mile from their future fenland home. From December 1942 until August 1943 they rented two rooms in a fifteenth-century farmhouse, Hellington Rookery. Then, finally, they bought a small house at Brundall overlooking the Bradeston Hills.

Ted, meanwhile, continued cycling to and from the Castle. He kept up his air-raid duties, still finding interest everywhere . . .

> Reed-maces produce vast quantities of fluffy seeds which blow about over the countryside and germinate quickly wherever they come to rest in wet mud. I remember bomb craters in Norwich which had a little water in them being exploited rapidly by both reed-mace and reeds during the war.

He saw the shining yellow flowers of Oxford ragwort, that formerly grew only sparsely on old walls in the city, now spreading rapidly among the rubble of fallen buildings. And a friend looking into an empty army pillbox saw. . .

> a group of ten peacock butterflies clinging upside-down on the ceiling; the insects were arranged in a perfect circle, facing towards a central space about the size of a halfpenny, from which their black folded wings radiated like petals of a daisy.

Several times, Ted's enthusiasm almost led to arrest when he was found poking about on bomb sites or in derelict buildings for bugs, flowers or — as he explained to one policeman — 'collecting woodlice'.

Ted was also collecting other things. He organised the Norwich part of a national appeal for horse chestnuts — used in the making of gas masks — storing them away by the ton in the dungeons, as volunteers, often including Phyllis, brought them in by sack-barrow from collecting-points around the city. The same volunteers also trundled sacks of vitamin C-rich rose hips up to the Castle, in further contribution to the war effort. As the collectors were paid small sums, books had to be kept — and that, too, was done by Phyllis.

By the time they moved to Brundall, Ted was writing regular gardening articles under the pseudonym Moldwarp — the countryman's name for a mole. What his readers didn't realise, however, was that their mole wasn't actually a gardener. 'He wasn't supposed to do any, because of his health,' Phyllis recalls. 'So he'd come in, and say — "Well, what have you done in the garden this week?" . . . and write about that. I remember one week our neighbours roared with laughter because in his column Ted said: "Now is the time to clean and oil your spades and hoes, and put them up for the winter." — Ours were still all standing about in the garden!'

Equally interesting to the neighbours was Ted's constant stream of visitors — some civilian, some in high-ranking military uniforms. Urgent questions sometimes couldn't wait for museum hours. On one occasion, a series of tragic deaths had occurred as landing aircraft crashed — victims of seemingly unpredictable sudden changes of wind direction. Air Force officers sought out the house in Brundall to ask for Ted's help. It took a leap of imagination to see the answer. Ted went to the Yarmouth tide tables and began to compare them with times of crashes. He was able to confirm his suspicion that in warm weather at low tide the vast exposed sandbanks of The Wash were creating a strong thermal, sucking air upwards. But as the tide came in, the rapid drop in temperature could reverse the effect and cause a sudden, dramatic change in the wind.

At Brundall, whoever the visitors were, they came in through the back door, because boxes of Ted's specimens were piled against the front one.

Jimmy, still taking pictures in 1941, snapped this brief reunion with *(left to right)* Percy and his wife Alice, Martin, Ted and Phyllis with Ted's mother

The back door opened straight into a crowded kitchen festooned with drying nappies, with a full-sized bath at one side, a sink, a copper . . . and usually up to five children running about, whilst Phyllis attempted to cook over an open fire. Mary, their first daughter, had been born in June 1944, and that year a friend, Alice, also came to stay with them, bringing three children aged five, four and fourteen months. 'We had to pretend she was my sister,' says Phyllis. 'People other than relatives were not allowed to come to East Anglia.'

Undeterred by the bustling domestic atmosphere, the visitors kept seeking Ted out. Another was a water company official. His problem was that gulls were perching on the edge of settling tanks and polluting the water with droppings. The men who in peace time had been employed to scare them were now gone. So Ted devised a system of spiked palings and loose, swinging ropes which successfully prevented the gulls from landing.

But it wasn't all work. There was time to go for walks on the Bradeston Hills. Three-year-old John went with him, hunting herbs for Phyllis when she was pregnant with Mary. And one January, John recalls, when the green slopes were transformed by snow, Ted and he took a sledge on the glistening toboggan runs. For a while the war was forgotten. On other days, from the hills, Ted showed him the 'doodle-bugs' (early German rocket-bombs) flying overhead.

Ted spent many evenings with another of his older teachers — a retired GP called Dr Deacon who, then in his eighties, still studied and cultivated hybrid plants in an enormous garden at Brundall — growing and selling violets and carnations. The old man needed little sleep and often kept Ted there, talking, until four o'clock in the morning!

There was also time for limericks. Ted, the story-teller and letter-writer, also needed little encouragement — throughout his life — to burst into verse. At this time he peopled his imagination with a host of characters invented for a series of 'Norfolk limericks', with his friend the cartoonist George Robinson adding illustrations. These are just a few of them . . .

> There was a young widow of Trowse
> Who most fervently worshipped her house
> On her much-polished hall
> All visitors fall
> That was how she got rid of her spouse.

> A mezzo-soprano of Lyng
> Got up at a concert to sing
> But stopped with a frown
> As the roof tumbled down
> When her voice made the rafters to ring.

> A waspish old whelker of Cley
> Once spat a large crab in the eye
> The crab didn't mind
> But returned it in kind
> And now the poor man has a sty.

Throughout this time they lived within a few miles of Wheatfen and continued to visit it. Then, in 1945, Captain Cockle died. On 14 December their second son, Martin, was born. The war's end brought another new beginning.

6 ❧ A home on the fen

fter her husband's death, Mrs Cockle moved to Margate and the Ellises were offered a lease on the dilapidated, damp pair of eighteenth-century marshmen's cottages and the 150 acres of fen that had been the Cockles' home. Then, days before signing the lease, Ted was offered a prestigious job, with much better pay, at the Imperial Mycological Institute in London. It would give him daily contact with other fungus specialists, plenty of time for research, good promotion prospects — and all the modern conveniences of a home in the city.

At Wheatfen, on the other hand, there was neither electricity nor gas. Water came from a well — it had to be hand-pumped into tanks in the roof if you wanted a bath — and the only light was from paraffin lamps. The house was bomb-damaged and it was half a mile from the village down a boggy track where no-one would deliver coal to them. They had no car yet they would be eight miles away from the low-paid job where Ted worked five and a half days a week. Inside, the house was so damp that a pair of boots left upstairs for a week grew mould. Outside, it was so wet that the tide once lapped the side of the house. And they had a new baby!

Needless to say, the Ellises didn't hesitate. 'With all its drawbacks, we wanted to live there,' says Phyllis. 'It was our idea of heaven. We didn't want to live in London . . . I would much rather cook on two Primus stoves and a haybox!' So live there they did — moving in in January 1946 without a second thought for the comforts of civilisation, fetching water in a bucket from the well, joyfully, in a continuous, grey drizzle. 'It seemed to rain every day from the time we moved in to the middle of May,' Phyllis recalls. So she dried nappies over an open fire fuelled with branches that she had dragged out of the woods and chopped up herself! About the only thing to suggest the twentieth century was a telephone.

'I remember John was not quite five,' says Phyllis, 'he got on one end of an enormous cross-cut saw, and between us we cut slabs from a bit of oak that was lying near the house. And we would go round the woods picking up sticks and things so that at least Ted could have a fire in his den . . . to keep his fungus collection aired!'

It was not the first time Ted had turned down impressive jobs. He had a growing reputation which brought him plenty of offers. The Natural History Museum in London sought him more than once, with offers of consultancy jobs or to run a department. In 1945 he had even been asked to go to Baghdad; an emissary was briefed to approach Ted offering magnificent terms — a specially built bungalow in the cool of the hills, servants and a large salary — if he would stock and run a brand-new natural history museum there. Like an earlier offer, in the late 1930s, to take up a post in Singapore, none of it tempted him away from Norfolk.

At first, Ted saw little of his new home. In those early months its scenery was shrouded in darkness by the time he returned home, by bus or on his shaky, unreliable autocycle. He went out in the evenings nonetheless, stumbling around in the moonlight or taking a boat onto the open waterways . . .

> Tonight a friend and I went off in a punt to enjoy the dark magic of the fen waterways for an hour or so. The night was strangely calm and cool with a small crescent moon peeping between high clouds. For once there was hardly a sparkle on the water; the Fen Channel lay like a sullen stream of lead before us and the little broads were cloaked in the shadows and reflections of trees so that they became mere blanks of mysterious space out of which only near objects loomed up in procession as we moved forward.
>
> We slipped past black hummocks of sedge and brushed black, snaky sallow boughs jutting out from the shores. Reeds, winter-pale, stood faintly glistening and ill-defined, merged with the dim, cloud-smudged skirts of the sky. The tremulous cry of a brown owl echoed across the valley and we heard the 'smee-oos' of widgeon gossiping in a hidden pool.
>
> From time to time a wood pigeon or a moorhen would be startled out of a bush with crashing wings, while loudly quacking mallard would resent our intrusion and rise heavily from the water ahead. One effect of the general obscurity was that for much of the time we were moving very slowly although I was using my one propelling oar vigorously enough. This was most noticeable when we were crossing the broads because we could not see the shores properly. We achieved a sense of speed only towards the end of our journey when we travelled along a dyke through the woods and could look up at tall trees against the sky.

Poor Ted was leaving for the smoke and bustle of Norwich before eight o'clock in the morning, and not returning until after six. One of those evening explorations almost brought his story to a premature end. Returning alone in a rowing boat, near Coldham Hall ferry, he was caught in a fierce storm. The surging, wind-whipped waters sank the ferry and his small craft was snatched up and carried downstream. Struggling to keep his balance, and far from help, it was three hours before an exhausted Ted

This pair of marshmen's cottages provided a dream home for the Ellises — a haven from which Ted was to work for forty years, investigating and describing the splendid surroundings

A trio of adventurers! Long before it was his home, Ted *(left)* set about exploring the damp acres of Wheatfen with Captain Cockle *(centre)* and specialists like E.A. Ellis *(right)*, the snail expert

reached shelter and safety. Phyllis only heard of the drama later; she had been at Brundall, completing the sale of their old house.

Wheatfen came complete with a resident tabby cat and, soon after, with the offer of part-time help from a countryman named Russell Sewell who had worked for the Cockles. He was to play a quiet, but continuing part in their lives for nearly forty years. He was a decade ahead of Ted in years and already had half a lifetime's experience of dyking, reed cutting, working on farms and as a nurseryman. As Ted was always physically frail, Russell was to take on much of the heavy work. He brought with him a special gift, for he, like Ted, had been fascinated by nature since boyhood, developing a detailed knowledge of his childhood surroundings. He had been born in that very house . . . one of a family of thirteen living there until 1907. He joined the Ellises in April and his first task was . . . cutting firewood!

Then Russell and Phyllis began the immense task of double-digging a half-acre of the soggy terrain, burying a layer of faggots and household rubbish to drain it sufficiently for the hard-up family to begin growing their own vegetables. At first working part-time, he became gardener, reed-cutter, woodsman, a permanent part of the family, and an extra pair of eyes for Ted. Russell, for example, could tell him that a particular clump of the tall, wispy purple small-reed — slightly overgrown with brambles — which Ted had noticed, had been there for at least forty years. A fen, too, has a life-story . . .

> A friend was telling me tonight about changes which have taken place in one of the small broads here during the past fifty years. The particular pool had, through the process of growing up, become isolated as a lateral bay by-passed by the tidal fen channel. Its waters were quiet and fairly deep, with an oozy bottom, and quantities of white water-lilies flourished there. It was also a great place for tench. Then a cut was made connecting its distal end with that of a neighbouring broad, and this at once introduced a circulation of tidal currents. In a few years the white water-lilies died out altogether, a different sort of mud began to silt up the pool and hornwort became the dominant weed; and tench ceased to inhabit the place as soon as their favourite oozy holes disappeared.
>
> This is just one rather interesting example of the way in which the Broads are known to have changed in character through human interference from time to time. Rockland Broad is said to have been adversely affected when the Claxton Beck was diverted to run into the Boat Dyke some years ago. There is no doubt that some serious mistakes have been made in good faith, as when the long line of wherries was sunk at Rockland with the idea of creating a scour in the main channel; the effect has been quite opposite.

Russell often accompanied Ted on his visits to other parts of the county. He became a favourite with the younger Ellises as well, and helped to encourage their interest in nature when, as was often the case, their father was

busily shut away in his study — by taking them to see odd patches of mushrooms, the place where the squirrel kept its nuts, or the spot where, at the
war's end, he had carved a 'V' for victory in the bark of an ancient tree!
Stories of the countryside were passed down through the generations by
word of mouth, so Russell could recount deeds of previous owners of
Wheatfen — and even showed the children rope-marks on some ancient
oaks said to have been made when timber was hauled out of the marsh to
make powder casks for the Battle of Trafalgar.

During those first weeks in his new home Ted had an extra task at the
Castle. He had encouraged his brother Martin — just returned from war
service in India — to apply for the job he had turned down. But Martin was
not a fungus specialist. Undeterred, Ted arranged to take him every day to
the museum and for three weeks gave him a crash course in the subject — a
curious 'abc' of spores and sporangia, mould and mycelium. Martin learnt
fast, applied, and got the job . . . eventually becoming Chief Mycologist of
what was, by then, called the Commonwealth Mycological Institute.

In May, not only did the rain stop but Phyllis's life was also made a little
easier when she was given a Florence paraffin stove with an oven. That
summer there came another turning-point when the *Eastern Daily Press*
asked him to write a daily article, to be called 'In the Country'. It was one
offer Ted did not refuse — and with good reason . . .

> For a great many years . . . under Archie Cozens-Hardy's editorship, John
> Knowlittle (until his death in 1935) contributed illustrated articles on Norfolk
> natural history at irregular but frequent intervals to the *EDP* and JK before his
> death several times told me that he hoped I would follow in his footsteps in this
> field. I was kept much too busy at the Castle Museum and in other ways to
> attempt this, but when eventually Tom Copeman's suggestion came my way,
> it was partly the remembrance of JK's wishes that prompted me to undertake
> this regular writing.

The column began on 1 October and continued for forty years — though
its original name lasted only two days, after which it became 'In the
Countryside'. And in his damp paradise, what better to write about on his
first day than . . . slugs! It was as if Ted were whimsically warning
generations of future readers that his poetic descriptions of nature's ways
would go down some seemingly unlikely trails, and that he was quite
prepared to speak up for some of the less romantic creatures, too . . .

> This has been a great year for slugs. They awoke early in the more than usually
> cheerful spring, then almost daily showers throughout the summer provided
> Utopian conditions for them, and they were able to glide over wet vegetation
> and eat away to their hearts' content by day as well as under the cover of night.
> Little wonder that the great black Arions grew never so huge and awful in the

79

gardener's eyes; now they have hidden their caches of jelly-eggs and their own days are numbered; this morning many of the fat old fellows which used to hunch their backs and rock from side to side when I tickled them lie like misshapen chunks of wet ebony out on the grass. The little milky field slugs are still busy, however, wreaking havoc amongst the flowers and ripening seeds of their favourite plants; by dusk I have seen so many high on the umbels of the marsh angelica that they might have been taken for clusters of gargantuan flowers fashioned by an Epstein.

Well, what else could be expected from a writer who, in 1960, must have brought panic to many of Norfolk's mothers with this gentle remark in his 'Young Naturalist' column:

> You will not be very popular at home if you make a hobby of collecting fleas and lice but I recommend it all the same, because there is no real uncleanliness about it and the small parasites associated with wild birds and mammals cannot live on people.

It was also in 1946 that Ted made his first − occasional — radio broadcasts. In a sense, however, his life's work now became the studying and recording of the life of Wheatfen day by day, almost growing to be a part of it. With a lifelong, unflagging sense of privilege, he came to regard himself as the custodian of 'millions of living things on my little fen'. He often seemed to feel that the place and his own life were woven together in a special way. David Bellamy once recalled a walk with him during which, suddenly, he was struck by the impression that Ted almost seemed to be 'growing out of' the bog he was describing. David told an audience at Norwich Castle in 1987 that, though he had met thousands of people, only once before — when he had been talking to a South American Indian tribesman — had he experienced such a strong feeling of a person having become part of his environment. In this intimate account, for example, Ted describes the life of a tree growing alongside him:

> In 1945 a very graceful silver birch tree on the lawn south of our house was blown down. In the following year one of its seedlings happened to come up in almost exactly the same place and we have watched it grow into a tree some twenty-five feet high; in a few more years it will be as fine as its fallen ancestor as the bark whitens with age. Throughout the years it has become the lodging-place of lichens and algae and the home of a great variety of small animals. Caterpillars blister and devour its trembling leaves. A rust fungus powders the leaves with gold before the time comes for them to fade in autumn.
> Tits and finches come for its seeds while they are still packed in slender cones. Summer warblers dart about its leafy boughs in search of looper caterpillars and tree-top-dwelling spiders. At various seasons the trunk is inhabited by slow-moving, shining brown mites, orange-red mites, which run fast on long legs, flat speckled bark-bugs, slender bugs which mimic resting mosqui-

toes, tiny caterpillars which build tubular cases out of lichen dust, bark ladybirds and other beetles, and an assortment of small midges.

On damp nights woodlice and springtails climb the trunk in search of green, powdery algae. Then there are all the creatures which use the tree as a resting place on sunny days, including stilt-legged flies and moths whose wings are camouflaged to match the brown and green and silver pattern of the bark. Today, when I happened to look closely at the trunk it was dotted about with dozens of minute, black moths which had white collars and glittering silver crosses on their wings.

The visitors started coming that first May, when the Association of Mycologists had a conference in Norwich and some members stayed at Wheatfen. The house was still bomb-damaged; two of the ceilings were hanging in strips and peppered the visitors' heads with dust each time they used the back stairs! Somehow, though, every visit to Wheatfen was made into a family occasion. With her new oven, Phyllis could make cakes, and Mary, in a sun bonnet, took them round on a tray as the fungus enthusiasts sat on the summer lawn, comparing the specimens they had collected from the woods. Not every group of visitors had it so easy, however. The arrival of the South Eastern Union of Scientific Societies in 1948 was often remembered by the Ellises — with a smile. The party, mostly elderly, arrived by motor-boat in order to get a lasting first impression of Wheatfen. They did!

Ted, with a sense of theatre, had taken a small sickle and single-handedly cut a half-mile path through the shoulder-high reeds — planning an impressive walk from the river bank through the heart of his marshy domain to the house. Phyllis, now with another young baby — Lucy, born in August 1948 — could not help. Came the day and, once more, came the rain.

The visiting zoologists and botanists alighted from the boat in a light squall, and stepped into several inches of mud. They then had to squelch their way — in a gathering storm — along a seemingly interminable route which they were in no mood to appreciate. The path was not even a straight one, for Ted and his sickle had veered and swerved around every significant clump of flowers as he made the path. As they trudged through the wet mire, Ted's enthusiastic voice drifted back to them, talking of 'tall, primrose-tasselled meadow-rue, yellowflags and valerian cushions of forget-me-nots', all of which were at the height of their bloom. But most of his words were lost on the wind, and the fifty bedraggled visitors, rain dripping from their note-books, finally arrived with relief at the back door. There Phyllis, ever practical, had prepared vast quantities of tea and scones, and set every fire in the house blazing. 'It seemed that every time you came into a room, there would be a small huddle of old men, with their trousers rolled up, attempting to dry their legs in front of the fire', she recalled.

That evening, at Yarmouth Town Hall, Ted attended their meeting, and was surprised to hear one of the speakers comment bitterly on the interminable mud and wet of Norfolk. Typically, his own written recollection of the afternoon was different: 'When the sun came out between two storms, they were rewarded by the sight of swallowtails in all their splendour beating away over the reed tops.' It seems you could have missed that if you had blinked!

On another famous occasion, Ted took a large party of about thirty — including several elderly ladies — on an evening walk which turned into a fatefully misguided tour: for Ted got lost in his own acres. To do so is quite easy. Even regular visitors are known to have become disorientated among the 150 acres of jungle-like woodland, winding waterways, carrs and reedbeds. It was not uncommon for the Ellises to send out search parties after dark for a missing researcher. Nor is it as funny as it sounds, because in places the deep mud creates 'quick-sand' conditions. His own children grew up with the rule, 'If you fall into the mud, spread-eagle yourself' (to prevent sinking). So the safest thing the embarrassed naturalists could do, as darkness fell, was to stay put. There they all stood, listening to owls hooting. Eventually they heard Russell — it was he, on this occasion, who came out — calling for them. He was able to lead the midsummer night's walk back for Phyllis's tea and scones . . . which they ate at one o'clock in the morning!

In their first year at Wheatfen the Ellises had started gardening, and Phyllis had an unusual 'pest' — a human one — to contend with. 'I remember he planted two rows of Roman nettles in amongst the beans — typical of Ted!' she recalls. 'On another occasion, I got into terrible trouble because he'd planted some wild garlic amongst my onions. I didn't know, and I pulled it up along with the onions!' Except for his interference with the flourishing garden, however, Ted's aim was to study, not alter, nature, doing his best to preserve and encourage the widest possible variety of habitats on his land. He didn't want anything to be 'tidied up'. As a result, his daily records were to chronicle, in miniature, a story occurring in many parts of Britain.

As Ted noted the arrival and departure of birds, the appearance and disappearance of rare plants, the fluctuating numbers of insects and yields of fruit, the variation in the types of fungi or lichens, the changing growth-rates of trees . . . he amassed an unusually vivid portrait of a countryside as it altered . . . partly through natural causes, but partly through the attacks of pollution from the air, changing agricultural practices, chemicals and detergents in the waterways, and increasing post-war tourist river-traffic.

Ted always carried a notebook when he went out, and the top pockets of all his jackets were visibly marked by his habit of constantly shoving a pencil into them, and pulling it out quickly.

His attitude to nature is beautifully illustrated by a decision he made soon after coming to Wheatfen. About the time Phyllis and Russell's vegetable garden was becoming established, he took a plough and ripped up one of their lawns . . . then patiently did nothing. The churned sea of mud stayed there and, predictably, weeds were soon flourishing with a vigour and profusion that would turn most gardeners grey. Still he did nothing except, just occasionally, a little judicious mowing. The effect of that was to simulate the natural grazing of meadowland by livestock, thus restraining some of the more dominant vegetation. Very slowly, then, among the vigorous weeds, a few of the more sensitive plants began to vie for a place. Over several years, by this purposeful restraint accompanied by gentle management, he created an area of natural Broadland meadow, with all the associated variety of flora — numerous spotted orchids, lady's smock, marsh thistles, knapweeds which attracted flocks of goldfinches when in seed, and sorrel which supported a population of small copper butterflies. All this . . . and he never sowed a seed!

Sadly, elsewhere the natural losses were often greater than the gains in those years. Looking back in 1961, he wrote:

In 1935, we had a rich aquatic flora, including water-soldiers, plenty of hornwort, frogbit, various pondweeds and quantities of cowbane floating in the corners. All these have vanished. There were marshes covered almost completely by broad-leaved sweetgrass which today are dominated by reeds. One fine piece of fen full of orchids and interesting small sedges and low vegetation is now largely overgrown by trees such as alder, guelder rose, sallow and birch.

The great saw-sedge *(Cladium mariscus)* was prominent in dense masses here and there. Now there is very little, owing mainly to the depredations of coypus. In 1935 the Fen Channel was narrow in many places and apt to become blocked by the floating beds of sweetgrass at times. Now it is wide and clear, and most of the floating grass cover has disappeared. New plants such as orange balsam have invaded us and new insects have become established, while many of the aquatic molluscs which abounded in 1935 are now comparatively scarce. Even the bird life has changed to some extent: Montagu's harriers no longer nest on the fen, but bearded tits have become resident in the area after a long absence.

Ted called the losses a tragedy and, though experts remain divided on the most significant cause, he — as the crystal clear waters began to grow muddy and grey — often attributed the main cause to the release of detergents into the Yare from the Whitlingham sewage works. That belief seemed to be supported when, in the mid 1970s, some, though not all, of the species were found to be returning after improvements were made to the treatment plant there.

In 1947 it had been a different story. A fierce winter devastated much of the wildlife — including thrushes, blackbirds and other fruit-eating birds, but mainly the smaller species, which were simply too tiny to withstand the intense cold. But then came a long, hot summer. Phyllis recalls:

'At that time the water in the channels was absolutely limpid and clear. You could see shells in the bottom, and fish. After the fish produced roe, in March, there would soon be myriads of tiny roach and sticklebacks swimming about in these clear waters. All through that summer, we took the children swimming and playing, sometimes by boat and sometimes walking across the marsh to the Fen Channel, where there was a hard bottom — an old road that had been made in medieval times for peat-carrying.'

The area could be equally magical at night. Early in March that year Ted took his young daughter Mary for an unforgettable journey on Rockland Broad. Over several days the naturalist had noticed a build up in the number of gulls that were amassing at night in the area. On one occasion a cloud of thousands appeared in the west . . . 'a dark, funnel-shaped mass resembling more than anything a waterspout at sea'. He guessed that they had chosen the broad as a vast, communal roosting-point. Eventually, one night, he and Mary went to see . . .

> On the night of 5 March, in a snowstorm which, for all its smothering, could not obscure the radiance of a nearly-full moon, we pressed our punt into service against a nor'-easter and a boiling tide and presently approached the gull roost. The birds were packed in a dense mass on the ice near the centre of the broad; none rested on the water of the shining 'wake'. They rose sullenly like smoke from a smouldering volcano and whirled above us in utter silence; we found it an eerie experience indeed. Then they began to settle again and, as we slipped away, had created once more the shadow island upon the ice which had dissolved so strangely a few moments before.

On another moonlit night, far out on the water, Ted and Russell were to meet something more sinister. This time banks of fog were drifting across the broad as they pushed out from the staithe into a silent world. Soon the shores were invisible, and they floated with no company but the soft splash of the oars. Then suddenly, in the bright moonlight, just ahead of them loomed two huge figures — like Norfolk giants — at least fifteen feet high, hunched in spectral manner over a ghost-boat. The apparition was coming straight towards them and made no sound. They caught their breath. Ted even ceased puffing the famous pipe for a spellbound moment. Then it was noticed that one of the monstrous silhouettes bore a marked resemblance to the Ellis profile. It, too, was smoking a pipe. For once, nature had tricked the naturalist — the moonlight had cast their shadows, hideously magnified, against a bank of fog as solid and clear as a white wall.

Ted *(left)* and Russell Sewell *(centre)* in the late 1940s take a winter journey to inspect the reed on Surlingham Broad. With them is Mr Sharman, another reed-cutter

From the first years the family supplemented their income by keeping pigs, bees and bantams. They also had apple trees and a sometimes-bewildering array of vegetables sprouted from the garden. Russell — an experimental nurseryman — liked to try out new lines, like Swiss chard or celeriac as soon as the seeds became available. Later, for a time, they grew enough to sell produce to, for example, the Assembly House in Norwich.

Also, in those days, there was still money to be made from reed cutting in the traditional way, by hand, during the coldest months between December and the end of February. It was a physically exhausting job that Russell had known since boyhood, and he continued to do it at Wheatfen, into his old age — stopping only in 1965. This occupation, too, was made a family occasion for the Ellises. Phyllis and the youngsters would don every available sweater and join in the gathering of the cut reed, which had to be carried in heavy bundles down to the water's edge for loading into their boat *Tar Baby*. Then, amid much cheering, the old boat, with water nearly over the gunwales, would ceremoniously chug down to Surlingham Ferry where the thatchers would be waiting with carts. Reed is a tough material, textured like sand-paper, and over the weeks Russell's hands would become hard, swollen and deeply cracked by the task. Looking at the annual ritual in his own way, Ted described it . . .

> The reed harvest is still in progress in this part of the Yare Valley and on the whole the reeds are good this season, for they made plenty of growth in the long, hot summer of 1949. The cutter's work is not so straightforward as one might imagine; indeed, it is often difficult to make up many bunches of uniform quality in any particular reed bed. Even at the water's edge, where the tallest and thickest stems are to be found, considerable patches are often spoiled by a smut which distorts the culms, and there may be reeds which look good enough but which are really soft, second-growth stuff which has followed the destruction of the prime shoots by moss grubs boring within them. Sometimes other reed-like grasses are present, and these have to be drawn out deftly with the point of the sickle as the cutter goes along, otherwise they would spoil the sample. On the more consolidated marshes, where the thinner-stemmed reeds grow, cigar-shaped gall growths inhabited by the grubs of a fly cause a varying amount of stunting, while here and there occur areas where the reeds have been attacked by a black rust as the result of infection from spores carried to them on the wind from buttercup leaves. Thus the cutter, winter after winter, takes his reeds where he thinks they look good enough to be worth his trouble, and leaves what is blighted. His action thus inevitably has a selective influence upon the pattern of marsh vegetation as time goes on.

Reedbeds dominate the marshland scene, vast acres swaying fluffily white with seed, or whipped and leaning to an autumn wind. Hardy as nature makes them, they are vulnerable to one special threat — fire. Dreaded by countrymen everywhere, an uncontrolled blaze can sweep through reed beds with terrifying speed.

In March 1948, it happened at Wheatfen. Ted plunged into a forty-acre inferno wielding nothing more than a sallow bough in a desperate attempt to save his woods, flowers, nests and the many creatures that lay vulnerable in its path. There were to be several times when the family fought blazes on the fen but this was the largest and most threatening. Wind whipped the flames as two separate conflagrations converged and moved over the reeds, threatening — in particular — a sedge fen colonised by rare swallowtail butterflies and bog myrtle. Birds flew through the columns of smoke in panic and jets of steam arose from marshy pulk holes as Ted and Russell tried to beat and trample along the leading edge of the fire. Recklessly, the naturalist kept pressing forward between outstretched fingers of the blaze, all the time risking being encircled by the fire. He hardly seemed to hear when he was called back. For four hours the two men beat their way along a mile-long fire-edge until, having started in daylight, night was black all around them as the last flames were put out. They trudged home over acres of sedge scorched down to its last, damp few inches. The butterflies, at least, had been saved and Ted wrote later:

> Having accomplished what at first looked impossible seems worth recording for the encouragement of others faced with a similar threat.

In 1949 Ted was unwell. His breathing was bad, but he would not see a doctor — perhaps dreading the confirmation of that grim news of 1940. He also had a lifelong fear of operations, telling Phyllis: 'That would kill me.' And so, it seems he just hoped for the best — seeking escape from this too-personal reality in his beloved fenland . . .

> Just after sunrise this morning, while the blue haze of night still hung in the valley and the first fiery beams were streaking the landscape with long shadows, I saw two herons standing like grey images in the very middle of a meadow. The birds had not come down by water for once, and I think they must have been on the lookout for moles, for there were hundreds of newly-thrown hillocks of earth all around them, so fresh indeed that their warm brown colour contrasted strongly with the crinkle of frost on ploughlands in the neighbouring fields. The herons were not sleeping, but poised and ready in all patience to make a deadly thrust at any heedless mole coming within range.
>
> They made a weird picture in the tawny cloud-light, and made me think of the crocodiles that lie in wait on the mud banks of the Nile at the moment of sudden dawn when little birds flock forth to breakfast. Then the sun shone more brightly and my attention was diverted to the flashing silver of an ivy bower, with its imbrication of leaves touched to the brightness of a dragon's scales. When I looked towards the herons again they were on the wing; they had observed my interest from afar and it seemed as though they had decided to move the moment I let them out of my gaze.

His health continued to deteriorate during that year. Mary, the oldest daughter, started school, and Lucy was now a year old. On 18 June he told his readers:

> I have been sent to bed for a time — how long remains to be seen — so that my glimpses of wildlife will be window-visions, or else they will arrive in the hands of children and friends . . .

He was ill for three weeks, continuing to weave prose around bunches of flowers or, as on one occasion, a baby cuckoo brought to him for identification. Then he seemed to rally. Allowed out, he made straight for the lawn on an errand of curiosity. For over a week he had been watching a cock yellow bunting from his bed, as it visited grass outside his window; this was not the bird's usual haunt . . .

> Today I was able to see that grasshoppers were the attraction. Doubtless these were being fed to the young birds in the nest not far away.

But in August Ted finally collapsed with a haemorrhage and doctors could no longer be put off. An examination showed his lungs to be ravaged by tuberculosis, and Ted found himself on a train bound for Kelling sanatorium, near Holt . . . writing his daily article on the way there, about the condition of railway embankment vegetation. There, he was told that he would, indeed, have to face an operation. Then a man on the same ward underwent similar surgery and died. In this grim climate, when the faces of visitors must have shown him their unspoken fears, Ted held on to his work — gleaning information from friends, or from the readers' letters which were forwarded to him, almost stubbornly determined to continue. A typical article begins: 'I am told there is a good crop of hazel nuts this autumn . . .' He noticed how often small birds — usually tits of one species or another — dashed themselves against the large windows of his ward. And he found that he could sometimes revive the more badly-stunned creatures with a 'a few drops of water put into the open beaks'. Eventually, they decided not to operate on him but Ted stayed there, seriously ill, until the end of January. It was then that they decided to ask Russell — still working part-time — to come and live at Wheatfen. Phyllis recalls:

'There was always someone elderly living with us — they took it in turns, a month at a time. Old Ethel had a wall eye, was fat and lame. Ted's mother had a broken hip and could not get around easily. Then there was my father and uncle, both of whom had bad hearts. I said to Russell one day: "I don't know what I'd do if we had a fire" . . . because we had paraffin lamps and candles all over the house. Who should I rescue first? Should I get the baby and children out, or the old people?'

So Russell who was living in overcrowded conditions, sharing a small bedroom with his brother, was found a room in the house.

When Ted, who stood only a couple of inches under six feet, returned home on 7 February, he weighed just over six stone. 'But worse,' said Phyllis, 'he seemed to have lost his faith in human nature. He'd had a very rough time in that hospital. He'd been the "odd bod" who got his leg pulled, and got laughed at. That's all right if you're feeling healthy — but if you're ill it's very hard to be the butt of sixteen other men. When he came home, he'd lost that lovely smile.' It was at this time that he wrote this poem, for Phyllis one of his best:

THORN ON THE HEATH

The thorn is dark up on the heath
This winter day
And the hill is crowned with a red fern wreath,
Raggedly gay.
The sun is silvered in a cloud;
The Wind is chill
And woods are wrapt in a sea-mist cloud
By Weybourne Mill.
The birch trees gleam in dancing light
Beyond the dell
Where they will stand like ghosts tonight,
Witching a spell:
A spell of beauty and of life
In mist and dark.
Yet the bent thorn's beauty, born of strife,
Is for the lark
That knows the freedom of the air
And nightly dies.
So when I look upon the fair
And face the wise,
The uplift' heart of the lark in me
Soars for the brave.
'Tis the crooked thorn I look to see:
Not the white witch-stave.

Ted's stay at Kelling had been a dark and lonely time — confined between four walls, regarded as an oddity, and the butt of jokes made about his patched pyjamas by men who didn't realise the well-known naturalist literally couldn't afford new ones. There had been times, however, when he had turned the tables . . . telling his room-mates, when they were served lentil soup that the lumps were 'a little worm', and promptly providing the worm's Latin name from his imagination. 'Never mind,' he added, 'it's all good protein!' On another occasion the matron sewed his bedsheets together in retaliation after he complained that the currant pudding had real flies in it.

Back home, there were other changes taking place. For Ted was still a 'spreader', as he had been from his youth, and Phyllis was a determined organiser.

'He had a study', said Phyllis, 'in what is now the dining room — a twelve-foot square room which was absolutely full of books, papers, letters . . . and

Taken shortly before he left Kelling; Ted *(right)*, shown with fellow-patients, is still smiling, but clearly gaunt and drawn

the corner of the ceiling had started to fall away. So while he was away, ill, I bought a little stove that would burn wood or coal, put it in the middle of the big bedroom upstairs — which is very much higher and larger, a much better room — with a chimney to warm it up, and put a day couch up there so he could rest. My father put shelves all the way round for his fungus collection and all the other boxes. We moved his big desk up there . . . and all the rest of his paraphernalia. So when he came back he had a much bigger room and much better conditions for a man with chest problems. And he was, of course . . . furious!'

Ted's anger over all his things being moved went on until a letter from his mother virtually ordered him to stop his 'megrims'. Peace was once again restored but many years later history repeated itself . . .

'He went to Crete in April 1971 and I found that he had again got into such a pickle in his big upstairs room that he was now having to work downstairs as well. Books were in piles on the landing. You couldn't even light the stove, because it would have been too dangerous. He had two big tables in there as well as his desk, and there were piles of books everywhere. So while he was away, I did the unforgiveable . . . and moved him again! I turned the children out of two rooms — one on the ground floor and one above, the two connected by the back staircase. I had the lower room completely shelved out for a library. (I happened to have a visit from the chief librarian at UEA at the time, who gave me advice.) We worked desperately hard, moving all the books and papers and getting them as nearly as possible into the order in which he had left them — better, in fact, because now there were no piles left on the floor!

'In the top room we had more shelves and an enormous cupboard — so that his boxes of fungi could all go in one place — and there were book cases and spaces for the other boxes. The big desk went up there, too. Of course, again we had 'megrims', and he swore he couldn't find things. I remember that when I had moved some of the piles off the floor, there under the old letters and papers I found the most enormous cobwebs I had ever seen in my life; I should think they were twenty years old!

'However much room Ted had, he still ended up working both on the table in our main room, and on the dining table at the same time. When we had visitors, I used to have to say: "Well, look dear — I must have a table." Otherwise, the rest of the time, we ate in the kitchen!'

During the time Ted was at Kelling Phyllis visited him three times a week. She usually went by bus after cycling into Norwich but occasionally managed to beg a lift. A few times she was able to find a driver to take the family's first car, a mid-1930s hand-built Triumph. If he was feeling well that was a treat and he could take it for a spin around the hospital grounds. Ted had passed his driving test in 1949 at the first attempt.

Over the years they had several cars; they were usually unreliable but that did not tempt Ted to take any mechanical interest in them. Cars, to him, were only interesting if they could say something about natural history. That may seem unlikely . . . but there were such times. When seeds sprouted in mud sticking to the foot pedals, for example, he examined them and noted that they were 'mostly of goosegrass and burdock'. Again, in 1961, it was a car that inspired his pen . . .

> We stayed at home today and set to work cleaning and painting our old van. The special enamel that we used dried rapidly in the sunshine, but not fast enough to save innumerable insects from being trapped in it. The glittering paintwork proved a great attraction to small water boatmen, which dropped out of the sky like tiny dive-bombers as they mistook the surface for water.

Other victims included two kinds of ladybirds colliding with the van accidentally, sundry flies which settled on the sunniest places by habit, winged aphids drifting by, a few plant bugs and beetles and a great many small sawflies.

In some places scientists make regular counts of insects, air-borne seeds, pollen and spores on sticky surfaces exposed deliberately as traps at various heights above the ground. This sampling of the smaller fauna and flora of the air often has its uses, especially in connection with the movements of insect pests and fungi causing disease in crops.

Ironically, whilst in hospital himself, Ted had been asked to undertake some medical research. For — in those early years of penicillin — he had pointed out that many other fungi have unexplored antibiotic properties. . .

Research has been almost wholly restricted to things easy to obtain in bulk, or easy to grow in the laboratory. Thus it has come about that many fungi which from their behaviour indicate that they possess highly developed self-protective properties, and many which have had long experience in breaking down the living tissue of plants and animals have not been exploited, simply because they are parasites or because they live in out of the way places.

Locating some of these 'out of the way' forms led to Phyllis crashing about in the darkness of the reed marshes that winter with a Tilley lamp, looking for the specimens he wanted to examine. Doctors were enthusiastic and offered to set him up with a bench and some equipment at the hospital. In the end, however, he was too ill to carry out the work.

Ted's illness added to their money struggles. He was off work for fourteen months, and on half pay for eight, before returning to the Castle in late August 1950. For three months that year, Phyllis had done some temporary supply teaching. Then, in 1951, she decided to work full-time and help support the family.

Just as he left the hospital, however, Ted was again offered a better-paid job. Again he refused it, this time on doctor's orders. The warden in charge of Flatford Mill nature centre, the Suffolk scene of Constable's painting *The Haywain,* was retiring. In June 1950 Ted was asked to take over, with inducements of free accommodation, free electricity, free coal and £800 a year. But doctors warned him that a change of job at that point could have endangered his recovery. It would also, of course, have left less time for studying or for broadcasting, and by 1950, Ted was beginning to be offered more radio work by the BBC. At the same time, students started coming regularly to Wheatfen. The first group, thirty undergraduates from Oxford and Sheffield, camped in the woods, spent a week doing research, invaded the local pub . . . and generally set a merry, boisterous precedent for future visits. Eventually eight universities took part in annual projects at Wheatfen. Ted would join the groups as they gathered around his log fire in the evening, to examine and comment on their work, or he would sit in with them on sing-song evenings at the local pub, providing spirited renditions of some of his Norfolk dialect recitations.

Until the late 1960s one of the regular student groups was a Southampton party led by Dr Joyce Lambert. Dr Lambert, an old friend of the Ellises, is best known for her work showing that the Broads are man-made, the remnants of medieval peat-diggings. 'You'll be telling me there's no God next!' one old countryman exclaimed when she told him. Her published evidence caused similar emotional disbelief, even abusive letters in the press. Ted was one, however, who defended her work . . .

> From time to time, widely-accepted ideas about physical features of the countryside are suddenly shown to be wrong as a result of scientific probing. For instance, geologists, geographers and naturalists all accepted the idea that the Broads were merely relict backwaters of a former estuary until . . . Dr Joyce Lambert made the startling discovery that cross-sections of Surlingham Broad provided unmistakable evidence of their artificial creation as peat-diggings. As it happened, I was the very first recipient of Dr Lambert's exciting news, since she came straight from the scene of her discovery to tell me about it in thrilling detail. I well remember her saying on that occasion 'Now I shall have to look at all the others [broads]' and, as we know, this promise was fulfilled with conclusive results.

In the late 1950s, the student groups had to be cut back following the discovery that their numbers and the constant trampling of the same tracks were seriously eroding the soil. At least one university, however, still sends annual groups.

The winter of 1953 brought a night of devastation on a huge scale, in a flood which left its mark on the Broads' flora and fauna for many years, as a salt tide crashed through the inadequate dyke walls and poured over fields and mudflats, drowning hibernating creatures and cattle alike on the night of 31 January. The calamity was repeated on other parts of the coast. Ted wrote of the incident in 1963 . . .

> I recall the adventures of that night only too vividly: how trees were falling across the roads, how half a straw stack was blown across my car and how a hail of frozen leaves stripped from evergreen trees smote me when I stood in an exposed spot. There is still a large yew tree standing in this village which was killed by the freezing gale that night.

Ted, in the thick of it as usual, was one of the first in the area to sense danger, due to his experience of living on a fen which is vulnerable to flooding. In his home dykes, he was puzzled first when water was sucked right out of the tidal waterways, leaving exposed mud. He phoned the chief engineer

A proud dad holds the final addition to his family — Suzie, born in November 1953. Looking on *(left to right)* are Russell, John, Martin, Lucy and Mary with Phyllis

of the river board who confirmed that 'big trouble' was on the way from the north. Then the waters began to rush back — in an unnatural way . . .

with alarming speed and I checked the level hour by hour . . . until it was no longer possible to wade through the flood to my tide gauge.

Ted, who had been dashing about the marshes and could be found anywhere between Surlingham and Rockland in those hours, was actually standing on the dyke wall when it broke a few yards ahead of him . . .

94

Water was pouring over the top like Niagara, and spreading out to form an inland sea over the marsh levels. It was a sight never to be forgotten. Only very rarely is the peace of East Anglia so shaken by the wrath of Nature.

Before the night was over, news was coming in of disasters and deaths along the coast . . .

and within hours of dawn I was looking at the newly created inland sea enveloping the Breydon marshes for as far as could be seen from Haddiscoe. Here at Surlingham, where the marshes are freely open to flooding from the river, my home just escaped inundation; but I realised that had it not been for the breaks in defences downstream we would have been immersed in swirling waters that night.

Suzie, their fifth, and last, child was born in 1953. In 1954 Ted increased his regular journalism when Stanley Bagshaw, a childhood friend, became *EDP* editor-in-chief, and started the 'Young Naturalist' column on Saturdays. In January that year 'Down Nature's Byways' was added as well. He was also writing a piece, 'Look Around With Ted Ellis', for a fishing magazine and regularly contributed to *The Sunday Companion*, a religious newspaper.

At the museum, however, he was becoming increasingly unhappy. Never a natural 'museum scientist', always happier in the field, it seems that Ted disliked some of the routine demands of an institution, and his personality clashed with that of the curator, Mr Roy Rainbird Clarke. The two men had known each other for many years. It was Clarke who had founded the Norfolk Research Committee in 1934 — a committee aimed at the inter-disciplinary study of the county's culture — which numbered Ted among its first members. It seems, though, that the museum brought out the different ways in which they saw achievement. While the curator, necessarily, emphasised the value of setting targets, and working towards longer-term goals, Ted cherished the freedom to pursue his sense of wonder whenever and wherever the moment took it.

One day, after a difference of opinion, he came home and told Phyllis: 'I think if I left the museum I could earn my living writing.' And so, in 1956, he resigned. Friends tried to dissuade him, but he stuck to his decision. The *EDP* commented that it was 'like Norwich City losing a gifted centre-forward'. Phyllis — though she says it was sudden, and had not been discussed beforehand — supported his move by agreeing to continue teaching until she was fifty. In fact, she continued until retirement.

7 ✿ Home life

n October 1979 Surlingham village hall was taken by storm with a surprise party to mark the Ellises' fortieth wedding anniversary. Highlight of the evening was an outrageous spoof of the Edward Lear poem *The Owl and the Pussycat* in which the Ellis children cheekily caricatured their parents. Ted (played by John) in a coypu fur hat and Phyllis (played by Susie) were shown arguing fiercely over the proper choice of a word: should the poem's boat be *pea* green or *sea* green? In the background, grandchildren Polly and Rose leapt up and down shouting 'BONG! BONG!', depicting a part of nature even Ted had never seen — the land (in Lear's poem) 'where the Bong Tree grows'. The revealing play was written and produced by their eldest daughter Mary.

Probably no scene better sums up the colourful, sometimes riotous home life of the Ellis family — where dictionaries were thrown down, like a challenge, in the middle of a meal as Ted, the communicator, and Phyllis, the school teacher, clashed over the usage or meaning of a word. It had to be settled then and there. They were both strong characters who argued often, but without bitterness. 'It was always up and over, like a bottle of pop', says Phyllis. 'But neither of us wanted to be a doormat. It was healthy!' Lady Enid Ralphs, widow of Norfolk's Chief Education Officer, recalls that even during tea on the eve of Mary's wedding, weighty reference books came out suddenly from far corners of the house when Ted and her husband, Lincoln, battled to probe the origins of the traditional nuptial rhyme — 'Something old, something new, something borrowed, something blue'. Why 'blue'? That time, at least, the text books were defeated.

Music was also part of daily life. The Ellis children learned to harmonise during communal singing over the washing-up. A piano stood in the main room, and all of them, at one time or another, played the recorder, violin, banjo or guitar. Ted alone could not play an instrument. But he made up for it; he sang, loudly, impromptu snatches of his own strange 'mock opera'. He sang in the bathroom; he serenaded whilst driving; when in a good mood, he yodelled all over the house. Although he could not read music, Ted enjoyed composition — and would warble home-made melodies to his own

poems. To suit his own high tenor, the tunes would always be in the key of F.
Phyllis would then write them down.

Huge family parties in the village hall were a regular event — with beer
and wine brewed by Phyllis (the yeast re-used to make ginger beer for the
kids), a wind-up record player and Victorian parlour games. Eminent
professors or bemused foreign visitors mixed in with villagers and found
themselves drawn into charades, or dancing on a diminishing piece of
newspaper.

Organising on a grand scale — taking a challenge — was in the Ellis
blood, and the children grew up in an atmosphere of 'anything is possible';
the maxim was 'If you want something to happen, go out and make it
happen!' As Sir Lincoln Ralphs — who was a family friend — once wrote,
'Ted's house is a powerhouse of interest and inspiration.'

In the summer there would be barbecues in the wood. Collecting wood
for the fire, however, was a perilous occupation, to be undertaken only by
the initiated. Woe betide anyone who picked up a dead branch or even a twig
that was hosting one of Ted's rare fungi! There were fallen trees at Wheatfen
that, deliberately, hadn't been disturbed for twenty years and, and though
Ted only rarely swore — with that gift for language he didn't need to — interfering with them was one of the 'crimes' that could provoke a withering
reprimand!

During the height of those summer parties Ted would sometimes take
small groups of his guests — many of them more used to the street lights of
town — into the real night, introducing them to the witching hour of the fens
that belongs to the shy, shadow-haunting creatures . . .

Towards the middle of the Broad, all oars were shipped and every boat drifted
very slowly so that all aboard might know the magic of the night. A thin sea
mist filtered the moonlight and bathed the distance in such a way that water
and sky became merged. This had the remarkable effect of transforming the
Broad into what seemed to be an unbounded inland sea, with here and there a
grey smudge of a reed clump or a thin black line of some island diminished to
the size of a floating piece of driftwood when viewed from a distance of a few
score yards.

The mist had a hushing effect on wild life. A solitary reed warbler chirred
briefly, a couple of herons growled at one another and there was a momentary
flurry amongst the coot. A redshank piped intermittently and the coypus,
usually very talkative by moonlight, cried out but twice in the distance.

Many bats flew in silence over the water; a lapwing passed over and a few
ducks hurtled by. Flocks of starlings slept in the reeds and when some of them
fluttered from one part of their roost to another on being disturbed, only the
sound of wings and hissing reeds came to us; there were no complaining
voices.

After the eerie voyage, a brief trek was made to a strip of fen where glow-worms displayed their little lamps in the dewy grass. One shining creature was placed in an open glass bottle for close examination. Within a matter of seconds, a male glow-worm, which is a winged beetle, had flown out of the mist and joined the lady with the lamp.

Or guests might find themselves carrying pieces of furniture upstairs to stand on in order to be shown . . . the slugs on the back of the wardrobe!

Usually in bed by about ten in the evening, Ted was regularly up by five — and often before dawn — in order to answer all his correspondence and go for a walk before breakfast. The early walks were a lifelong pleasure from his Gorleston days. He said he did his best work in the slumbering dawn hours and he loved the mists, the hush and the orange-lit clouds of early day . . .

> Those who feel enslaved by the turmoil of their days might well try early rising and so come to savour the enchantments of first light on these summer mornings, especially if they live out of town. Even in the midst of a city like Norwich, this magic of gentle awakening prevails, with dew sparkling on leaves and flowers and a fragrance unsullied by petrol fumes lingering in the air.
>
> Today, I strolled but a short way across my fen-and-woodside garden into a fairyland of tall grasses nodding with the encumbrance of overnight rain-drops. Most of the buttercups were still closed and leaves of white clover were only just beginning to unfold. Two fresh mounds of rich crumbly soil showed that a mole had been busy just before my arrival.
>
> I listened to the purring of turtle doves, the mournful cooing of wood pigeons, the trilling of wrens and the harsh utterances of a whitethroat. A flock of swifts passed low overhead at speed, heading Norwich way. A jay flapped across the fen and three black-headed gulls came over from the east.

Back in the house, at breakfast, he would usually tell the family what he had dreamt. Ted dreamed vividly all his life, and took great interest in these sleep-visions — either amused by their surreal sequences or pondering their deeper meaning. The importance he attributed to them stems from his belief that he had occasional psychic powers and that there could be communication between certain minds. For, along with the dreams, he sometimes experienced strong sequences of pictures and scenes passing before his eyes as he was on the point of sleep. Sometimes dramatic or disturbing, they seemed occasionally prophetic — as on one night when, it is said, a Yarmouth man who sometimes brought him specimens suddenly appeared before his sleepy eyes. In the vision, Ted saw that the man was thinking about coming to the museum with a fungus sample. The picture was clear enough for Ted to identify the fungus he was holding, so he pulled himself out of his reverie and jotted down its Latin name. He had that piece of paper with him next morning at the Castle when the man walked in . . . carrying exactly the right fungus!

Never short of visitors: *(left to right)* Martin, Lucy, Phyllis and Suzie share a pleasure trip at Wheatfen with a family friend, Pat, and Bill Howell, one of Martin's pals

Though Ted became used to such occasional experiences, he didn't always find them pleasant. On first coming to Norfolk as a ten-year-old he was badly upset by discovering that he 'recognised' a Yarmouth house, and knew, accurately, the appearance of its rooms without ever having set foot in it. There was also another occasion, in Ireland, when an older Ted came to an unfamiliar village and knew where a particular shop would be.

After breakfast Ted would either resume some particular piece of research, write an article or prepare for a broadcast. When he was at home, however, invariably he would bob up — smiling — at noon at the door of Coldham Hall, the local pub. It is said that you could set your watch by him. He would arrive on his bicycle, often with Russell, and usually clutching a bag of scraps for the ducks. After Ted left Kelling sanatorium, doctors had advised him to drink beer, to help him put on weight. It doesn't seem to have been an unwelcome suggestion; he always enjoyed a pint and, because he was not a heavy drinker, quickly became (believe it or not) even more enthusiastic and talkative.

On one occasion, out filming, Ted was already in a naturally joyous mood when the crew stopped at a pub for lunch. He began to entertain the customers with some of his comic songs and Norfolk dialect recitations. This led to his being bought several more halves than he was used to. In the afternoon, Ted was due to interview another naturalist. He was supposed to prompt his guest with just a few questions but when the interview started, he talked without pause for twenty minutes — unstoppable — while the bemused interviewee sat in front of the camera trying to get a word in!

A beer company once considered using the well-known duo of John Mountford — for long his television 'partner' — and Ted to advertise a new ale. But they dropped the idea when market researchers found that the public did not associate Ted with beer. The naturalist laughed out loud when he heard the news, telling John: 'You can't *be* a countryman unless you drink beer and smoke a pipe!'

So the bar at Coldham Hall was for many years his social club, a convivial release from the solitary nature of his work. During the winter, in earlier years, the snug became the venue for a pensioners' get-together, a lively haunt with Ted serving behind the bar. One old regular sat in the same seat each day and watched the sun move round on the floor, pointing out with great exactitude: 'That's beginnin' t'alter . . . That only came t'here yesterday.' Another old boy, perhaps following the habits of a lifetime of accurate regularity would watch the clock and sip his pint at precise five minute intervals and by continuing in this way would finish his pint on the hour. Then he would order a second and proceed in the same fashion.

Before long, Ted was boosting trade. Visitors would come just to see him. Characteristically he was always helpful and could often be found pulling pints behind the bar in a busy moment, or popping outside to take someone across the ferry, which was also run by the pub. The autographs that he handed out in the years of fame were usually embellished with a lightning sketch of a bird or a fish; and he was not only willing but keen to talk to any stranger, generously buying drinks, gleaning new information from them, and pouring out his love for his subject to one and all.

Harry Last, for many years the landlord at Ted's local, has a copy of his book *The Broads* typically doodled with a sketch of a swan's head, beneath which appears the inscription: '*Cygnus bibulosus* [Latin for "boozy swan"] . . . stainless variety peculiar to the River Yare in the immediate vicinity of Coldham Hall. Has never been known to touch Guinness out of respect for the landlord or . . . possibly for fear of capsizing.' Harry's favourite drink was Guinness, and in the late 1960s a tame swan, affectionately known as Fred, did more than live in the vicinity; it used to join Ted in the bar for a drink and a packet of crisps.

Landlord and regular became good friends during that time but Harry, who came to the pub in 1922, remembers a much younger Ted from those very early years — not as a drinker, but as 'a thin little chap' coming over the ferry from Brundall in the 1920s, sometimes with Arthur Patterson. 'He was just a young chap then. He always had a sack with him, and he would disappear into the marshes and then — at the end of the day — we would feel quite sorry for him . . . we would see him coming back, dripping wet, and the sack would be full of specimens.'

In later years Ted would often give his celebrated impression of a laughing jackass as he left the pub — a party piece he had learnt long ago at Keswick Hall. In fact, he had a little-known gift for animal impressions and, though he never claimed to 'speak the language' like a real-life Doctor Dolittle, he was close to it on occasions. Ted could charm a passing cuckoo down with his call. He once wrote about one that seemed baffled and sat on a branch looking about for the rival it thought it had heard.

There was also his 'poacher cry' which, though it was heard but once, has never been forgotten. On certain nights at the height of the season Ted used to enlist friends to patrol his fen and discourage poachers. On one crucial night, however, he was alone, so he used his imagination instead, and decided on some mischief. By chance, it was the night of the full moon, and with this in mind he crept out alone to the edge of the woods. There, hidden in the shadow of the trees, be began to . . . howl! Ted let out a wail so piercing that it seemed Norfolk's primeval wolves must have returned. He kept it up for half an hour, baying at the moon and filling the fen with a sound like the Hound of the Baskervilles. Phyllis, in the house, heard the poachers' dog whimpering, and men stumbling, crashing and cursing in the undergrowth . . . as they made off in pursuit of a new career!

In gentler ways, he developed his own rapport with wild animals, writing once:

> It is often said that a pheasant knows who is carrying a gun and who isn't; also, that it recognises Sunday as a day of rest, and is not long gaining confidence when shooting has ended for the season. I suspect that there is some measure of truth in all these notions, but what I have learned by observation is that many birds, including some pheasants, react very differently to different people approaching them. There seems to be a happy medium as far as walking is concerned. Stealthy movements evoke fear and suspicion, while sudden erratic actions cause alarm.
>
> Without any invitation on my part, I have on several occasions had small birds settle on my head or shoulders, in an exploratory fashion, and I have a vivid recollection of a waxwing swooping down from a tree to hover only an inch from my face as it inspected me. It also helps to gain the confidence of some birds if one talks to them gently; at least, it excites their curiosity so that they linger awhile.
>
> There are red squirrels in our woods, here, but for many years I have had only fleeting glimpses of them. Today, however, I wore a brown duffel coat

with a hood to match when I went for a stroll and, when I encountered two squirrels, they performed a wonderful series of acrobatic games quite close to me, and I really felt that in my strange nut brown, almost furry garb, they took me for nothing more fearsome than a wandering deer.

Having the ability to make birds land on your head isn't always convenient. It happened to him once when, the house full of guests, he slipped outside discreetly to obey a different 'call of nature'. Whilst standing by a bush, contemplatively, he was perched upon by an owl.

Everyone who knew Ted agrees that there was nothing false about his demeanour when he appeared on television. He walked in front of the cameras and was simply himself. On screen and off, Ted liked people and the casual visitor who spoke to him in the bar at Coldham Hall was just as likely as any old friend to be invited back for a guided tour or a meal. If this happened, though, you could be surprised by what you ate. For years Ted really had worn that coypu hat featured in his children's play — popping up among the reeds like a latter-day Davy Crockett. But turning them into headgear isn't all the fen-folk did with the plump, lank-haired, South American creatures once they began infesting the Broads. Russell shot them by the hundred and took the long, reddish-coloured front teeth to the pub, where they were in demand as lucky charms. The Ellises, never vegetarians, made pies and casseroles of them.

> I can speak from ten years' experience of eating and enjoying coypu *en casserole*. My wife prepares them as follows: joint, discarding the offal; wash thoroughly to remove long hairs and strip off superfluous fat; dust with flour and fry lightly to brown on both sides. Next, chop up one or more onions and fry. Put all in a covered casserole, adding herbs to taste (thyme, lovage, parsley and bay leaf, salt and pepper; or chopped celery, turnips and carrots, and a trace of garlic salt). The merest dusting of powdered nutmeg and clove can be recommended. Cover with water and cook in a moderate oven (250 – 300 degrees Fahrenheit) for three hours or more. The result is something like veal; sometimes the resemblance approaches chicken and at other times, depending very much on the accompanying herbs and vegetables, coypu would pass simply for rather superior rabbit.

Contrary to popular myth, however, the Ellises never ate coypu for Christmas dinner ('We were never *that* poor!' says Phyllis), but they did often serve it to guests. Lady Ralphs was one — her verdict: 'It was a bit like rabbit.' Ted once played a gastronomic joke on the august members of the British Association for the Advancement of Science when they visited Norwich in the mid-1960s — by arranging to take charge of the meal and, secretly, serving them all this local delicacy.

Typically, though, Ted was also one of the few to find something positive to say about the destructive creatures which became hated vermin on the

Broads. He looked closer, studying them in his thorough way, researching their eating habits, and even learning to imitate their calls. Whilst not condemning the necessary extermination measures, he pointed out that they were not so destructive, individually, as some of our native mammals. He met them on many occasions, and, getting closer to them than most people did, once wrote a beautiful description of coypu at night on the fens:

> When coypu swarmed everywhere in the Broads they could be heard calling to one another all night long, rather like lowing cattle. The moans of some were pitched distinctly higher than those of others, but whether the females were more shrill than the males, or the young took time to acquire a deep and lusty timbre I could not discover. When hunting along the Fen channels at night, I was sometimes threatened by *basso profundo* growls uttered by large coypus sitting hunched on the shore. The sounds they made were rather like those of snoring barn owls in ivied towers, ghostly and menacing. Once only I found myself witness to the gentle crooning of a mother coypu, surrounded by her young. She was humming a delicate lullaby, little louder than a whisper, but as musical in its way as the singing of grey seals on a sandbank in the pupping season.

Coypu was not the only wild fare to find its way onto the Ellises' table, for they often ate fungi too; Ted, who specialised in their study, also became a connoisseur of their varied flavours, claiming that the rest of us do our taste-buds a disservice by sticking to the commercially-cultivated mushroom (though Ted, of course, unlike most of us, was expert enough to recognise and avoid poisonous forms). The Ellises have also been known to serve up snails, rooks — and once even tentatively tucked into a grey squirrel; this proved so tough that even the dog couldn't eat it! Their gastronomic experiments extended to both common garden snails and banded hedge snails, but . . .

> I cannot in honesty say that they were worth the trouble taken in preparing them for the table. For the most part their muscular little bodies proved rubbery in texture and intrinsically they possessed no tastiness such as one finds in winkles.

Though not much of a cook himself, Ted did know his herbs, and developed an unusual flair for serving up a tasty, traditional, old-English style of salad, blending the herbs with vegetables . . . and also flowers. Even the family's wine could be unusual; they made it sometimes from the rising sap of birch trees.

If Ted took hospitality seriously, it was also a lifelong point of principle with him to reply personally to every letter he received. His broadcast 'Nature Postbag', for example, aired only a small selection of his weekly mail. The rest he scrupulously took home and answered, believing — 'If people have taken the trouble to write to me, I owe it to them to reply.' In view of his popularity, it was a creed which caused him hours of labour. But even when the BBC offered to send brief, polite letters of thanks on his behalf, Ted wouldn't hear of it.

The BBC's regional radio signals from East Anglia took his voice to Lincolnshire, Northamptonshire, Huntingdonshire, Cambridgeshire, Norfolk, Suffolk and Essex. But, with networked broadcasts as well, he received mail from all over the country — even from abroad, for he was both remembered by emigrant East Anglians who would write to tell him about other worlds of nature, and admired by foreign readers who had been sent his cuttings or books.

The letters asked him everything under the sun and were sometimes strange: what to do about an oiled bird found on the beach; do coconuts give blue tits indigestion; how soon can you expect nuts from a young tree; what causes a toad to spawn in autumn instead of spring; why do birds kill themselves against window panes (a frequent one); where to see otters; how to keep honey bees out of a jam factory; how to recognise deadly nightshade (another common query); how long do birds live; how does a ploughed field come to be covered suddenly with gossamer; why would a heron peck a cow's tail; is it true that it 'rains' frogs; and . . . what is this luminous centipede that I found in my bed? Of course, the letters, and frequent phone calls, were often repetitive, but he never seemed to grow impatient, was always pleased and interested, and had the ability to make the questioner feel they had helped him. There were, not surprisingly, regular correspondents — fellow-enthusiasts who became pen-friends over the years . . . men like George Crees, of whom Ted wrote at his death in 1970:

> His interests as a naturalist were balanced and he discovered many things which had escaped previous notice, such as the predation of the eggs and nestlings of bearded tits by water shrews. His letters to me came at rare intervals, but they were always deeply interesting and rich in original observations.

The general public did, at least, receive clean writing paper, but with closer friends, he was more informal. Ted kept a stack of old sheets on which he had typed his articles before they were phoned to the newspaper office; this pile of paper was usually given a second lease of life . . .

'Ted used to pen his letters on the back of old typed *EDP* paragraphs,' recalled the Reverend Sir Alan Webster, a long-time friend and former Dean of Norwich. 'So a rail journey from London with views that morning of pastel silvery estuaries might be the notepaper for down-to-earth messages: "chattering flocks of fieldfares" and "magical lanes with withered meadow-sweet" on one side, with the problems of making the Rayburn work on the other; "the winter iridescence of resinous trees in the sun's reflection like Aladdin's wealth of jewels" on one side, arrangements to meet in the after-noon on the other.'

Ted's den, as he called his jumbled, packed study, was one of the undiscovered wonders of Norfolk. 'He must have had a remarkable memory just to be able to find things in it,' said Dr Joyce Lambert. It was dominated by a seemingly limitless number of cardboard boxes, the size of shoe boxes, packed with more than 10,000 microscopic fungus specimens — each individually wrapped in a piece of used typing paper, neatly folded and minutely labelled. Every shelf in the room had been filled long ago, which meant that books, scientific journals, more boxes, odd fossils, jars, letters, slides, discarded specimens, and drawings lay scattered about the floor in a chaotic form of order that only Ted could understand.

No-one was allowed into the room — especially not to clean — and at one end of the desk, on the floor, could be found a peculiar pyramid-shaped heap looking, at first glance, like dry soil. It was the spot where he habitually tapped his famous pipe as he mused over the microscope, a script or a learned article . . . and a growing accumulation of old pipe dottle marked the passage of weeks. He lived in chaos — as far as Phyllis would allow him — but nothing delighted Ted more than to discover that his mass of papers and dust attracted their own natural denizens . . .

> While I was sorting out papers today I came upon several very elegant and diminutive pink spiders *(Oonops domesticus)*. When disturbed they made no haste to dart away and I had to tickle them a bit to induce them to move at all; even then they walked reluctantly to the edges of the papers from which I was able to dislodge and deposit them out of harm's way. My den is a paradise for the pink *Oonops* and they are cherished guests, earning their keep by destroy-ing the booklice which are always turning up among my books and specimens. Booklice, for their size, are extremely powerful insects but the spiders hold on to them tightly even if it means taking a brief but rather hectic ride pick-a-back until the insect's struggles cease. Each spider has a small home cell to which she retires and where she lays eggs only two at a time at intervals throughout the summer.

Tobacco tins were everywhere; he used them not only for tobacco, but as depositories for mosses, insects, berries — anything, in fact, that he hadn't already stored in an old matchbox or a typewriter ribbon container. All of these were pressed into thrifty service as containers for specimens. His pockets were therefore usually bulky with several tobacco tins and, of course, the inevitable was bound to happen. Engrossed in a car journey conversation, he once reached for the wrong tin . . . and smoked half a pipeful of dried-up insects before he realised what the strange smell was. It was a pity, because he had just made a special journey to collect them! One shouldn't be surprised that Ted was slow to realise his mistake on that occasion, because he was known not to be too choosey about his pipe-weed. If caught short in the woods — especially if he needed a smoke-screen to ward off biting insects — he would scoop a fill of dried catkins or leafy fragments.

Ted once, in 1948, successfully grew his own tobacco and when he came to harvest his crop he was fascinated to find evidence that — as he always claimed — tiny creatures are not so bound by instinct as we imagine; they experiment, too! A species of enterprising spiders had explored the unfamiliar leaves and adopted them as a suitable substitute for their usual 'nursery'. He found hundreds of eggs and was naturalist enough to refrain from picking the affected leaves for a month until the youngsters hatched.

> To dry the great tongue leaves, I spitted them like rows of herring on reeds laid across beams in a stable.

Immediately, there was more evidence of nature's adaptability . . . as hordes of drone flies found winter lodgings among the drying leaves. It seems a pity, after so much effort, but the truth is that the fumes of Ted's home-grown were strong enough to clear the top of a double-decker bus. After a few pipefuls even he gave up and put the bundles into 'storage', where they lurked untouched for some years.

There is no doubt that occasionally Ted could be the 'absent-minded professor' type. He was a walking fire hazard and seemed to possess no clothes that were free from little burn-holes. He had that unfortunate habit of putting the pipe into his pocket before he had put it out . . . Anxiously watching out for smoke rising in his wake was a family preoccupation.

In striking contrast to his den, however, was another quite different room that Ted had arranged with almost military precision. It was lined from floor to ceiling with library-style corridors of shelving and nothing was out of place. This room housed his collection of over 4,000 books, which included many rarities — the oldest being an edition of Dodoen's *Historie of Plantes* translated by Henry Lyte and printed 400 years ago. Books were the essential tools of his trade, the complement to that remarkable memory, enabling him to weave strands of far-flung experience into his broadcast replies and his writing. Thus, when commenting on the occurrence of a golden-coloured blackberry at Runhall in 1948, he was able to say: 'A similar plant was found by a Mr Jacob Bobart in a hedge near Oxford a few years before 1724.'

Shut away for much of his time in his den, or browsing in his private library, there were times when Ted felt cut off from family life. John, his eldest son, recalls how Ted would bring drawings out to show to the family, as if he wanted them to share in what he was doing. Or he would rush into the room, excitedly, and shepherd his children in, one by one, to look through the microscope at a minute, exquisite fungus growth on a dead spider. Very often there would be a hurried, impromptu family slide-show as soon as his latest pictures came back from the developer.

One of Ted's favourite family activities was collecting the blackberries which Phyllis would make into pies and jams. He conducted the exercise, of course, like a scientific experiment — weighing the fruit, keeping records and comparing yields year after year, as in this note from 1960:

> The wild blackberry crop is as heavy this year as it was in 1959, although the berries were three weeks later in ripening . . . there has been far less damage inflicted by wasps and flies this year, to offset the slightly higher incidence of grey mould on over-ripe berries.

Throughout the years at Wheatfen, every Sunday morning Phyllis would cycle or drive to Surlingham Parish Church where she was not only a regular attender but also played the organ. Ted, after the choirboy days, was never again a regular church-goer. He often gave his services to raise funds — as he did for other village institutions — but, privately, he was not a Christian. If asked about his beliefs he would sometimes politely side-step the issue with a half-humorous reply such as 'Oh well, I used to be in the choir, you know.' Though he seems to have believed that a part of the human spirit survives death, he became wary of specific creeds, telling his daughter Mary: 'We don't need a Heaven — it is all around us!' and, on another occasion, saying to his youngest, Suzie: 'I don't believe in reincarnation; you, my children, are my reincarnation.' As well as having five children of his own, the man who had watched so many life-cycles come and go on the fens was also eventually blessed with eight grand-children: Suzie's Rose and Tom; John's Richard, Matthew and Clare; Lucy's Jesse; and Mary's Polly and Emily.

Yet many friends assumed that Ted was a Christian, and some of those who knew him well still describe him as a 'religious' man. In a wider sense, he was, and saw something in nature that he found difficult to express. Speaking to a journalist in 1986 he referred to it as

> A sort of spirit of life. . . . I'm not a total adherent to theories of the origins of life and the way things have evolved. I think that it has all come through . . . you have to say the 'emotion', the 'imagination'. I'm putting it in crude terms but there is in the heart of the life-substance this spirit of adventure and experiment in response to what happens. And this is how progress has been made.
>
> Without such an explanation, I think you cannot explain the extraordinary bridges that have been jumped by . . . parasites, for example, which spend most of their time on grasses or pine trees and then in the Spring, go through a stage which is essential to complete the life-cycle in some quite different plant — you know, an orchid or whatever. So all these things have come through an 'inner spirit for change'.

Writing in 1976, he put it another way:

In contemplating the face of Nature we are constantly reminded that the quicksilver of life on earth was making magic long before our time.

If Ted was sceptical about some religious certainties because of his closeness to science, he could equally be sceptical about some scientific certainties because of his closeness to the 'quicksilver'. In 1978 he wrote a newspaper article which, for once, was concerned with nature as a whole, rather than small parts of it. The article was entitled 'Music of Nature':

It is the fashion for those who describe the achievements of science to insist that inventive genius is nurtured by pure logic and a coldly objective examination of physical and chemical processes.

Any idea of what is loosely termed 'emotion' tends to be rejected as a negligible factor in the evolution of plants and animals and the progress of human technology. I am constantly surprised that this assumption is made by people purporting to be dedicated to a search for truth, because all living things from the beginning have achieved change by trial and error according to their environmental experience. Living, for a microbe, a man or a tree, is an adventure during which many emergencies have to be coped with. How individuals react to various challenges may be important for their survival long enough to reproduce their particular brand of stamina in some of their offspring.

Sensitivity to external stimuli does not account for all progress, however. Without initiative and experimentation there could be no change. In animals, large and small, a complex sensory equipment is involved, with a consequent increased scope for behavioural interplay. In the course of this interplay vital advantages may be seized, but the decision to seize them is determined through emotional reaction rather than objective calculation. How else can adaptability be interpreted? The gorgeous nuptial display of the peacock, the flashing messages of glow-worms and fireflies, the droning of the mosquitoes, bird song in spring, the colours, scents and shapes of flowers invite emotional response.

A scientist may dissect organisms down to the very elements of their cell chemistry and genetic essence, but he is dealing with mechanisms. What is thought? It is something more than mechanical computation, surely? From it comes creativity and change, with all the intricacies and ornaments of the living world, including attractants and repellants, evoking pleasure or fear as the case may be and ever blazing new trails to glory. A poet rather than an astronomer speaks of the 'music of the spheres'; it is the poetry inherent in sentient beings which has been responsible for creating what we call music and all that is embraced by the term 'beauty', out of the rhythms of the universe.

Some time around 1972, the Japanese scientist Hiroshi Meguri — the man who discovered the layer of plankton under polar ice — came to the

University of East Anglia for a short time. He contacted Ted simply because he had seen, and liked, the series of Jarrold colour guides to the countryside which Ted had written. 'Where can I get the whole set?' Hiroshi asked. He got more than that; in the brief phone call Ted discovered that the foreign scientist would be in Norfolk at Christmas and had no-one to stay with . . . so he was immediately invited to Wheatfen. There Hiroshi found himself in the midst of a cosmopolitan party including relatives, friends from the village, and a woman visiting from France. He phoned his wife on Christmas Day from a house noisy with children, dogs and violin music. On Boxing Day he was helping move the furniture out of the main room . . . to make space for still more guests!

Ted and Phyllis presided over such pandemonium with accustomed ease, for their home was always like that. Ted was on first-name terms with most of the well-known personalities in his field — from David Bellamy or Johnny Morris to Peter Scott. Some of them visited him. So did dozens of men and women who, though not media figures, have names equally familiar in their fields.

Wheatfen was always an 'open house'. For his children, the things that went bump in the night at Christmas were often more visitors arriving, late, by the car-load with Ted. They got so used to finding up to six strangers in crumpled sleeping-bags on their bedroom floors, at all seasons, that the kids dubbed them collectively 'the refugees'. People arrived, as if by magic, while the children were asleep, and looking to see who was in the latest sleeping-bag could be almost as much fun as opening presents. Sometimes they found an eccentric scholar with more letters after his (or her) name than you could write around a Christmas stocking, sometimes a student, and sometimes refugees in the literal sense, for Wheatfen hospitality has been extended to exiles from Poland, South America and, once, to a Ugandan princess who stayed, virtually in hiding, during the height of Amin's persecutions. Throughout the time that he worked at the museum Ted had run an international household, with guests from Holland, East Germany, Sweden, America and the Middle East.

If it was Christmas, no matter how many arrived, Phyllis always made sure that everyone had a stocking — sometimes making up a dozen or more, by an almost biblical feat of provision, in the small hours. Ted, especially in the earlier years, would have been busy in his own way outside, hours earlier, cavorting in view of the windows dressed in a Father Christmas outfit.

The festive season at Wheatfen was old-fashioned, with its own traditions. One was to join in carol-singing with other villagers on the nights leading up to the holiday. There was church on Christmas morning, then a country walk. Ted, of course, would have walked miles already in the dawn hours. In 1951, when that famous curiosity got the better of him, he narrowly avoided the fate of a brandy-doused pudding . . .

A nice crisp, sunny day tempted me a bit further afield than usual on the marshes. I came to a spot where great gobs of gas kept rising from the ooze as I walked through a bed of rushes. I thought it would be interesting to see if the gas would ignite, so I held a match to a nice, large bubble as it popped out of the slime and burst. It was like setting fire to methylated spirits. I was enveloped in a sheet of blue flame that set fire to my coat and the surrounding rushes. Fortunately, it was soon snuffed out but I haven't tried the experiment again!

Later in the day Ted would distribute the brightly wrapped parcels — but in his own fashion, just one at a time. He regularly told his children they would enjoy Christmas more if they shared in the pleasure of other people's presents, too. 'So it was like a lucky dip,' says Suzie, 'and it went on for ages! You might get three presents in succession, then you might have to wait half an hour.'

In the evening there was a move towards the piano, with Phyllis at the keyboard leading a rowdy, sometimes tipsy, grand sing-song, aided by anyone who was still capable of holding a fiddle or a banjo. The singers always gathered up the last of their strength for a spirited rendition of *Jerusalem*, bringing the evening to a close on a note almost — but never quite — loud enough to arouse the many small creatures snuggly hibernating in Ted's skirting boards, attic and walls.

Such hospitality was not confined to Christmas — it went on all year round at Wheatfen. There was rarely a week without extra places set at the table. A visitors' book would have filled half a shelf, but that sort of formality would have been unthinkable; the guests were never allowed to feel like 'visitors' for long. A tea-towel would be thrust into your unwary hand or an empty bucket for well water hoked over your arm with a casual informality which made everyone part of the family. Phyllis could be heard yelling 'Come on, Dr What's-Your-Name, have another sausage,' bringing a note of commonsense practicality to the most scientific debates. Tim Wyatt, their marine biologist friend, tells a typical story . . .

'I moved to East Anglia in about 1967 and must have met Ted in the winter of 1967–8. I can remember the night well enough if not the date. It was thrashing with rain, gusty, pitch black. Naturally, there were no locals about, and I became increasingly incredulous of those bold enough to open their doors on such a night and provide directions, the more so as the village lights were swept away behind me in the gale. When I reached what I subsequently learned was Tuck's Wood, the track disappeared entirely. Then I recalled a muddy turning that I had previously dismissed as probably leading nowhere and, besides, unnavigable under the conditions

Traditional reed cutting, now rarely seen, was still a familiar activity in the 1950s. Both Mr Sharman *(right)* and Russell *(centre)* had lifelong experience of this arduous work

then prevailing. Nonetheless it was "the way that I went", and it led me to a magical world.

'Ted and his family had created a home with all the charm of that built by

111

the Swiss Family Robinson in the story which Ted had heard as a small child on his mother's knee. That was the way in which he himself regarded it, but I prefer to liken it to the wonderland of Christopher Robin, complete with the debris of dolls and other toys which his children had scattered in every room.

'Many visits followed. I would arrive, usually impulsively, sometimes feeling like an intruder before entering the house, but always sensing a warmth that a member of the family might feel once I was inside. I remember evenings of eating and talking and laughing, of doing my turn at the kitchen sink, of spontaneous music which Bob Copper himself might have envied. I remember hordes of other visitors who were all made equally welcome, that there was always a bountiful stream of stews and bakes and crusty bread, however many of them arrived, and the tiny cantankerous stove from which Phyllis coaxed it all.

'If we all decided to trudge off into the woods or marshes, there were always enough gum boots, cupboards of them waiting for walks. The house was completely occupied by the activities of the inhabitants. As well as Ted's collection of books and specimens and notes, there were paintings and costumes and a thousand other signs of prolific minds. Chatting with Ted in his den, enveloped in clouds of tobacco smoke, one might hear the sound of Martin's banjo or Suzie's and Lucy's fiddles, or hear Phyllis cussing the stove or ransacking the freezer as another car-load of visitors arrived.

'I remember "holy hour", when Phyllis dictated the day's "reflections" to the Press by telephone; and Russell sitting quietly in his chair, or teaching me how to grow leeks; and afternoons with Martin persuading a water-logged punt . . . into the swampy heat of a windless day on Wheatfen Broad, later scouring the jungle for fuel for an evening bonfire in a clearing in Surlingham Wood, with files of people carrying pots of beans and sausages and jugs of home-brew along the twisting trail; and a great box of toys emptied onto the floor for stray children; and a tree-house in an oak at the edge of Wood Carr whence one might scan the marshes and the skies or watch the flight pattern of birds and listen to the wind.

'Over the years that I knew them the children of Wheatfen flew too. I think John was already in the Navy. Martin went to Sweden and France and Wales, Mary to London, Lucy to Liverpool where, unbelievably, she met children who had never seen trees — Suzie to Newcastle. In these years I remember spending long hours with Ted learning about the lives of snails and spiders, of sphaeroma and microcyclic rusts, about pollination by insects, and pipistrelles and the gummy exudates of alder leaves and much, much more.

'Ted's early exposure to the artificial and romantic assembly of the Swiss Family Robinson had soon given way to the real worlds of wonder described by Darwin and Wyville Thomson and other nineteenth-century naturalists.

He gave me, and I have it by my side now, Wyville Thomson's two-volume *Voyage of the Challenger,* a voyage regarded as one of the cornerstones of modern oceanography. Ted's microscope, still in use when I knew him, was from the same era. Ted also gave me A. H. Patterson's manuscript, *Fishes of Norfolk,* which was never published. I returned it years later when I learned that Ted regarded himself as a disciple of Patterson. But books and instruments and microscope preparations were only an introduction to this aspect of Wheatfen. The real treasure was Ted's knowledge and understanding of nature, and the ease with which he imparted it. To see beauty in a patch of decayed reeds, or scum left hanging on a twig by the receding tide, or in the squelchy brown mire of a pulk-hole — that takes a very special power of observation. To convey it to others takes a special kind of mind.

'Eventually the children began to drift back again. They brought another generation with them . . . then the house was full again of shouting and laughter and music, and cupboards full of tiny boots were found so that the children could enjoy squelching with the grown-ups. Now they can discover the joys of weedy dykes and cracking ice with sticks and the thrilling sounds of a gale lashing tall trees or a bumble-bee looking for a place to make a nest. I wish I were one with them now!'

The guests certainly came by car-load and even by coach-load . . . as on the occasion when fifty piled out one lazy afternoon, and Ted, standing behind Phyllis, muttered 'Oh yes, I think I forgot to tell you they were coming'. The visitors still got tea and cake, though no-one is quite sure how she managed it. Many a research student engaged in long afternoons studying the fen discovered it was impossible to slip away, past the house, without being spotted by Phyllis and ordered in for tea.

To a child's eyes, too, some of the gifted visitors were memorable. Who, out on the marsh, was that big, bear-like, square-shaped man with a beard, who sat silently for unbelievable ages just bent over a tripod with his old-fashioned plate camera hidden under a black cloth? 'Look at him! He doesn't seem to move! He scarcely seems to breathe!' They weren't allowed to go near him. And if they asked why, Ted whispered that he was trying to take a photograph of . . . a spider. Then there was the fungus specialist who would appear regularly, once a year . . . disappearing with their dad for days on end, the two of them returning to cram the house to over-flowing with soggy bits of smelly toadstool, reeking lumps of mushroom, bits of mouldy wood, damp slivers of rust-eaten vegetation, as the season's cull of specimens was lovingly spread out to dry on pieces of newspaper that covered the tables, perched on the stove — you couldn't even find free space in the airing cupboard!

It did gradually dawn on his children that their home-life was unusual. Brought up without television, Suzie used to eavesdrop on the 'Did you see

Ted, in his coypu hat, with Phyllis. The family call this picture 'Punch and Judy'!

that last night?' conversations at school, then repeat them, pretending she had seen the programmes too, so as not to feel left out. They still lived with bucket toilets, Tilley lamps and well water for long enough to be able to introduce college and university friends to the archaic scene on weekend visits. 'I think it was only then that I really saw us as other people did', says their son Martin.

On one occasion General Washington-Platt, a descendant of the famous American statesman and for many years a family friend, invited the whole fenland clan for a meal in Norwich's plushest, most exclusive hotel. 'Phyllis had tried to smarten us up', says Martin, 'But we still had our clothes tied together with string. We must have looked like hill-billies!' The youngest, Suzie, sat goggle-eyed. 'There was so much food!' she recalls. 'I couldn't get over the potatoes; they had little sprigs of parsley on them, and I couldn't believe the amount of butter they were swimming in! We lived very austerely and if you had a little bit of butter on your potatoes, it meant a *little* bit!'

Hospitality at Wheatfen wasn't reserved just for human guests. There was a time when visitors had unpleasant instructions to stop on the way there and pick up the remains of any traffic-squashed roadside creatures as food for a young, injured owl that Ted was nursing. Often the house came to resemble an animal hospital and, though he never claimed to be a vet, nor encouraged people to bring him such animals, he found it hard to turn away forlorn casualties when friends, and even sometimes total strangers, turned up with them at his door. Others were brought to the museum, and occasionally Ted would find an injured creature himself out on the fen. And so there were owls, field mice, a bittern in the engine house, a heron (with one leg) in the hall, a red-throated diver, bats . . . . It is said that Phyllis drew the line at gulls, yet . . .

'I remember we had gone to make a short film for 'Weekend' about what life was like in an ordinary day for Ted,' recalls John Mountford. 'I wanted to go to the bathroom and I heard a strange noise coming from inside. Ted said: "Be careful as you go in there because I've got a little friend staying." There was a full-sized gull rattling around in the bath! "Oh yes!" he said. "Someone brought it for me to look after. I've got to get rid of it before Phyllis comes back or she'll be furious!"'

The injured owl was called Wol and had exclusive use of one of the best rooms in the house, liberally spread with newspaper. Nor did anyone use the hall while the one-legged heron was staying, as that part of the house took on a strong aroma of raw fish. On another occasion the family had to stop having baths for several weeks when the tub became home for a skua, another gull-like bird.

The bittern, found injured by Ted, took over the engine house and there made a strange spectacle of itself; the shy creature was nervous of unfamiliar hands and reacted in the only way instinct suggested — by trying to hide. Bitterns are giants among fenland birds, and rely on camouflage to conceal themselves. Even now, when the result had become absurd, its elegance had to be admired. For there stood the bittern, in the middle of the concrete floor, surrounded by mechanical clutter and ramshackle shelves, stock still and silent, the long neck and beak gracefully pointing straight upwards . . . every feather concentrating on an attempt to resemble a clump of reeds! As the season turned, and the bird recovered, another bittern could be heard booming in the distance of the marsh and the captive began to answer. Realising it had found its future mate, Ted was able to time its release to give it the best chance of survival.

The ever attentive Ted even took pains over his household slugs — deliberately leaving out treats of cheese crumbs and milk for them in damp corners. Most people might not relish a slime trail on the floor but Ted was always delighted; he knew that the yellowish-brown house slug, sometimes up to two inches long, is becoming a rarity in modern homes and deserves protection. This night-rambler lives in gaps behind skirting boards and similar holes. So human guests at Wheatfen were warned to watch where they were treading if they got up in the small hours. After a warning like that . . . they usually did!

Ted had also discovered the little-known fact that house slugs are partial to cocoa. Once he knew this he indulged them with offerings of the beverage and his little friends thought they were in slug heaven. How he found out about it is not recorded, but how one of his guests found out is known. The young man curled up in a sleeping-bag on Ted's floor one night with a nightcap — a mug of cocoa. It was asking for trouble but he wasn't a student of slugs. Being tired, he dozed off and left the cocoa half-drunk beside him. In the morning he awoke to his own private natural history lesson: there, as plain as day, were several fat slugs swimming and gorging themselves in the cold cocoa dregs!

8 ❧ Rusts and smuts

t was not until well into the 1930s that Ted began the collection and study which became his consuming passion and, as he said with characteristic modesty, 'dared to specialise' in a field previously dominated by academics. In fact, he was to become an authority on the unlikely subject of plant diseases and parasites — especially the minute fungi commonly known as rusts and smuts.

Typically, what started him looking at the blotches and weird growths that most people regard simply as blights was the discovery that, if you really look, they are beautiful! In an account of a fungus foray he went on in 1958, he wrote:

> I spent most of the time there crouching among rushes and moor grass in a hollow near a clump of alders and concentrating attention on the smaller gems of the fungus world. One of my treasures had the appearance of gold lace encrusting a bleached stalk of marsh horsetail; it had all the brightness of yellow pollen, spilled from a bee's pollen-basket.

Many fungi — and Ted specialised in the smallest, the microfungi — need good eyesight even to spot them; and it takes a microscope to appreciate their delicate structures. Ted had and used both. When he looked through his microscope at that find he made on the 1958 trip, for example, it inspired his pen still further . . .

> The rich gold threads looped loosely about the horsetail are fruit bodies of one of the mycetozoa, *Hemitrichia serpula,* a species never before found in England, although it once appeared on rotten wood in a glasshouse in the West of Scotland. It has prettily netted spores, and elater threads with spiral bands and prickly-looking hairs.

Discovering that rarity was just one of the many successes his specialisation brought him. In 1961, recalling its beginnings, Ted wrote:

> I have made a special study of plant diseases for the past thirty years and have made the acquaintance of thousands of different kinds of small fungi during that time: rusts, smuts, moulds and so on.
> The strange thing is that when I was a boy, I cannot remember having

noticed these things, although I was interested in insects, wild flowers, birds and things that lived in water. How was this new world of tiny fungi opened for me? I happen to remember how it all began. One day I noticed some bright orange pustules on a wild rose stem in spring. They were very conspicuous and when I looked at the orange powder under a microscope, it proved to consist of a mass of glistening round spores.

I sent a sample to an old friend who was an expert on plant rusts and he not only took the trouble to tell me the name of the fungus, but told me how later on I should look out for beautiful black, stalked spores produced by the same fungus on the rose leaves. So I was introduced to the complicated and interesting life history of a common plant rust.

From that time onwards I looked more closely at all kinds of plants and found that most of them were attacked by fungi, both when they were alive and after they had died down. It was simply a case of 'getting one's eye in'. Now my friends think I must have what they call a 'jaundiced eye' with which I look round their gardens and discover diseased plants, but it is only an extra interest, really.

In keeping a sharp look-out for micro-fungi parasites, one meets with some interesting problems. Some very common plants have rare diseases and certain fungi turn up only where the host plants grow on a certain type of soil or live near the sea. If you start hunting for these things, you will soon become fascinated by them, as I was.

The old friend who inspired Ted was Arthur Mayfield of Mendlesham, who pointed out to him that to the fungus-hunter dead vegetation is as interesting as the living plants. The fascination lasted and, in 1951, it was in recognition of his outstanding work on microfungi — discovering them, recording them in various habitats, studying their life histories through inoculation processes and experiments, and so on — that Ted was elected a Fellow of the Linnaean Society — the oldest natural history society in the world.

In youth, once his attention had been drawn to their beauty, it was typical of Ted to find his curiosity deepened by a sight that to many of us would be unappealing . . .

Many years ago, at Gorleston and along the high banks of Breydon Water, I used to be mystified on finding numbers of the common, yellow-brown hairy dung-flies clinging dead to the spines of spear-thistles. My first thought was that the spears might somehow have been responsible for the death of the insects, which were not, however, actually impaled on the prickles. Then I saw other flies in similar plight on the heads of grasses and on the undersides of the leaves of various herbs and bushes and realised that some disease must be rife among the insects.

Nowadays I am familiar with similar diseases attacking not only flies (including gnats and daddy-long-legs), but also mites, sawflies, earwigs, caterpillars, aphids, plant bugs and beetles, and know them to be caused by special fast-growing fungi, the Entomophthorales. The spores of these fungi get caught in the hairs on the insects' bodies and there germinate, sending outgrowths into the breathing pores, which become choked with masses of mycelium and bring about death in perhaps two or three days. Showery weather in June seems to suit such fungi.

Once he had started his quest for fungi, armed with the same microscope he had used since boyhood, Ted soon found them everywhere. He was sometimes modest enough to say that he was making new discoveries just because no-one had bothered to look for these things before. For many years, however, it is a fact that most of the entomogenous (insect-attacking) fungi added to the British list were his discoveries — meaning that he was the first to find them in this country, though some were known abroad. He also found some which were completely unknown. In December 1950, for example, a collection of aquatic fungus spores made from one dyke at Wheatfen produced fifteen species, including six that could not be matched with any known examples. He published an account of these with Professor C. T. Ingold in the *Transactions of the British Mycological Society* — still imbued with that youthful sense of magic. . .

> We have one particular pet . . . with four-tailed catherine-wheel spores which are so strange and beautiful as to capture the attention of any microscopist.

Another of Ted's fungus finds, though not one of his beloved microscopic ones, now rests in the British Museum. In October 1958, at Holkham Gap, his sharp eye lit on a diminutive earth-star; it proved to be *Geastrum minimum,* the smallest of its group to occur in Britain, and the only authenticated example then known in this country.

In a field which requires intense specialisation, however — one man might spend a lifetime studying insect parasites alone — much of Ted's contribution to science has come through collaboration. He was known in the scientific world as a generous and helpful man always willing to make suggestions and pass on an interesting specimen. Many a specialist has received a small parcel through the post with a typically cryptic message from Ted attached to the contents: 'Here is something interesting — have fun with it!' In many cases, the fun has yielded research papers, sometimes with an acknowledgement of Ted's help and sometimes without. A paper by the late Mr T. Petch, for example, in *Transactions of the British Mycological Society,* describing some extra large spores as a new variety of *Empusa forficulae,* was based on material sent by Ted who spotted it infesting earwigs on cabbages growing in a garden at Old Lakenham in August 1944. The two fungi which have been named after him, *Microscypha ellisii* and *Nectria ellisii,* were both described in this way — through work by other specialists on material found by Ted.

Ted's special interest was the smallest parts of nature — many of them invisible to the naked eye. *Top:* he is pictured with his treasured microscope, 'the bride', a boyhood gift which linked him to generations of past naturalists and first opened his eyes to the intricate beauty of tiny forms. *Right:* This photograph of fungus growth on a dandelion leaf shows one of the less 'romantic' aspects of nature which so fascinated him

Even in this climate of scientific collaboration, however, it is likely that much of Ted Ellis's contribution remains completely unrecorded. But in a field in which jealousy, plagiarism and preoccupation with the building of personal reputations are not unknown, Ted was regarded as a trusted figure who would give freely of his thoughts and creativity to aid another's work. Both among local naturalists and further afield, he was sometimes an 'uncle' figure, someone to discuss your ideas with and, though not a specialist in every field, his unusual breadth of knowledge helped him to forge links and put the specialists in touch with each other. More than one scientist, after perhaps only a brief conversation with Ted on the way out of a meeting, has been surprised by a phone call days or even weeks later, saying: 'I've been thinking about what you told me . . . have you thought of . . .?' And if a colleague was ever feeling jaded, Ted could always be relied on to restore flagging enthusiasm and reawaken a sense of 'these rich adventures'.

Equally important to his scientific contribution was his life's work of caring for his creatures and natural habitats at Wheatfen. For he encouraged others to use it, study it and carry out original research on the small things there as well as the large . . .

> The variety of wildlife is much greater than is generally understood. This is because the attention of most naturalists tends to be focused on the more obvious and well-publicised things such as birds, mammals, reptiles, flowering plants and butterflies and moths. Although a great many naturalists' societies exist in this country, published histories of the flora and fauna of various counties tend to overlook the wealth of 'lower' plants and invertebrate animals, partly because only a few specialists devote attention to them, and partly because the numbers of species involved would be likely to prove an embarrassment for the editors of journals catering for majority interests.
>
> One result of this situation is that many so-called county natural histories, even where Norfolk is concerned, are in reality very limited in scope and too grandiose in title. Overmuch attention is concentrated on the better known things, so that relatively trivial matters concerning them occupy precious and costly space in our journals, while plant and animal groups advertising very significant roles in the countryside are seldom allocated more space than the simplest recording of their listed names demands from time to time.
>
> The balance will not be redressed until far more enthusiasts turn their attention to the cultivation of interest in the smaller forms of life and set out to make their discoveries interesting to a wider circle of naturalists and other people. I try to do this myself with the fungi, which are tremendously various, far more numerous than our flowering plants, extremely interesting in their adventurous adaptions for survival and of great significance ecologically. Algae, many orders of insects, worms, rotifers, mites, spiders, myriapods and crustaceans suffer from a similar scarcity of champions endeavouring to reveal the wonders of their existence and function in our midst. They present a wealth of opportunity for naturalists looking to a fuller future.

It was Ted's passion — and his genius — to look, and see. In a sense, that prevented him from becoming a 'scientist' in the modern sense; his methods and his accuracy were scientific but he remained by choice the inheritor of a Victorian tradition — a field naturalist in the line of the great amateurs. The statistical research, laboratory work, formulation and testing of hypotheses, or the repetition of experiments, which are all part of modern science interested him only rarely. For Ted, there were always too many new things to look at! But what he saw he described with such detail that his work provided rich raw material for others more concerned with such questions as the taxonomic relationships between fungi or their evolutionary development.

From his first days at Guernsey and throughout all his youthful rambling, Ted was inclined to look at the whole of nature — at how the lives of animals and plants at a particular place and time influence and even depend upon each other. 'Ecology' is now a fashionable word, but it was not so in 1925 . . .

> Round about the beginning of the present century a new-fangled word, 'oecology', began to be bandied about by a few of the leading botanists here, following the lead of Continental workers who were striving to build up a new line of study directed towards the scientific interpretation of the pattern of wildlife in the world, as related to the climate, soil and association of various kinds of plants and animals in particular places.

Ted wrote that in 1949, citing Professor A. G. Tansley's pioneering role in the ecological study of plant life in Britain. It described an approach to the study of natural history that was already a principle for Ted by the time he was first exploring Norfolk. Percy Trett, now a respected amateur marine biologist in Yarmouth, used to accompany his own grandfather — a lay preacher friend of Arthur Patterson — in those years. He remembers the teenage Ted's advice to him: 'Go for ecology!' Ted urged him not just to look at one group of animals or plants but always to consider the whole picture. Percy also recalls Ted advising him, 'study humans . . . they are animals too, you know!' Fifty years later Ted was passing on much the same message to another generation in his 'Young Naturalist' column of July 1975:

> Singleness of purpose plays a very important part in deciding the experience of a naturalist on any excursion into the countryside. I have found on various occasions that if, for instance, my interest at a particular time lies in searching the undergrowth of a marsh for the fungus parasites of insects or spiders, which are mostly white, I will find numerous specimens. If I am thinking mainly about plant rusts, I will notice them and probably very few insect parasites will catch my eye. Sometimes I set out to assess the general picture of vegetation in a certain habitat and will register only the presence of flowering plants. An ornithologist will see and hear birds and register their presence

with skill and patience, although he may afterwards have no recollection of passing butterflies or the variety of flowers brightening the scene.

However, if there is concentration on one thing one day and something else on another day, memory stores a kaleidoscope picture of the living world so that anything new and strange leaps to the eye. The importance of disciplined observation in many fields cannot be over stressed. Curiosity must be fed at all times by a quick resort to every possible aid for explanation of any observation which happens to excite interest. There remain countless mysteries to be solved by individual initiative, and whatever one's chief interest may be, it will always be better for enlargement of experience and the acquisition of knowledge outside the field of specialisation.

Nature is an integrated whole, and it is impossible to appreciate the behaviour of birds, or insects, or slugs and snails, or fungi, without paying balanced attention to the plant world in which they operate and on which their lives depend. So no excuse is necessary for a wide-ranging interest in natural history.

At times, Ted's discoveries of fungi took not only keen observation but endless patience — as in this detective story:

> When I was spending my summer holiday going round some of the Broads in my punt a few years ago, I went ashore at Martham one day to look at the insects and wild flowers on a little patch of rond marsh. On examining the purple marsh orchids growing there, I found that they had dark brown circular patches of some kind of fungus growing on their leaves. Later under a microscope I could find only the network of thread-like strands of the fungus mycelium attacking and discolouring the leaves, but there were no spores or anything in the way of fruiting parts of the fungus.
>
> My books had nothing to say about such a parasite on marsh orchids. A year or two later I found the same fungus at Sutton Broad, but had no better luck in finding a name for it. Then in 1935, rather later in the year, I found little pale brown spores being produced in branched aerial sporophores at the edges of the brown patches on marsh orchids at Horsey.
>
> It was now possible to recognise the character of the fungus more clearly. Its fruiting branches and spores were very much like those of the very common olive-brown mould which grows on all sorts of newly-dead plants out in the open and which is called *Cladosporium herbarum*. This summer I have made absolutely sure that the orchid fungus was a parasitic kind of *Cladosporium* and there is a very good chance that it is new to science.

That was in 1955. The sample would then have been sent to specialists for examination and laboratory testing. As late as 1985 Ted was making new discoveries in the world of tiny fungi — even as near home as his local pub where, in December that year, he spotted a 'measles'-like growth on blue-green oat grass in the riverside garden as he passed by. With the pocket magnifying glass ever handy, he noted:

The leaves were sporting brilliant orange-red, circular blotches on their upper surfaces, while small, shiny, black, shield-like specks were visible underneath.

With all thought of beer put aside for the moment, he collected a sample and later wrote that that particular pathogen seemed not to have been found previously in this country.

Ted's most famous piece of detective work came through a leap of imagination. He regarded it as a highlight of his career, for it demonstrated his unusual feeling for what should be found together at a particular place, and led him to postulate the existence of an unknown fungus. Later his prediction was proved to be accurate, yet at the time the fungus had never been recorded anywhere, and its first discovery — in America — was still to be announced. Ted already knew that most catkin-bearing trees take part in one of nature's precise games of 'time and opportunity' — when the spring's falling catkins become infested with spores which will not reach maturity for a full year, just as the next season's catkins drop. During that time these spores protect their hosts by investing them with a kind of chemical armour, so that they become 'mummified'. Next spring, the spores take on a different form, developing into long-stalked, brown 'cup fungi' just before they produce the new generation of spores. That, he knew, was the story on catkins of alder, sallow, poplar and hazel . . .

> It used to puzzle me that no such fungus was known to have a connection with the catkins of bog myrtle. It seemed to me that there really ought to be one.

Unbeknown to Ted, at that very time, an American researcher was writing a description of a new fungus he had discovered in the USA on maple . . . and on bog myrtle! Ted, having made his guess, visited Askham Bog in Yorkshire and collected specimens which proved him right. A week later he found the very same fungus on bog myrtle at home. It was a year later before the American's discovery was named — *Ciboria acerina* — and Ted was able to confirm that it was the same species as the one he had found. He commented proudly:

> I regard that as a triumph of the imagination.

His work on micro-fungi ranks amongst the most important of Ted's contributions to the study and appreciation of the natural world. Indisputably there were many others, but two seem worthy of particular mention here: first — as the mycologist Peter Orton says — was 'his work on the advancement of Norfolk and, indeed, East Anglian natural history. He made many new friends for the area and had a phenomenal knowledge of what was to be found in Norfolk and where'; and second, his role as a 'defender' or conservationist. Considering him in this latter guise, however, it is sometimes difficult to understand why Ted — a man who knew so much of nature, and who had chronicled the man-made damage better than most — did not protest more often in the interests of conservation? He had the facts at his finger-tips and could say not just that 'certain species are declining', but knew precisely where, when and how many in relation to his own land. His fame undoubtedly gave him power to influence public opinion yet, generally, in his broadcasting and writing he kept a low profile — maintaining an impression of gentle good humour, the enthusiasm and wonder seemingly unruffled by a campaigner's axe-grinding or by bitterness in the face of materialistic spoilations. The truth is that he was actively concerned but didn't think shouting — or, at least, frequent shouting — in the media would help.

It is less well-known that, from his earliest years at the museum, Ted was an active member of various committees in Norfolk concerned with pollution and conservation — such bodies as the River Board Pollution Committee, the Broads Advisory Planning Committee, the river authority, the Broads Society, the Broads Authority and various committees concerned with maintenance of specific nature reserves. His concern for conservation featured strongly, too, in his decisions to join the Surlingham Parish Council and Forehoe and Henstead Rural District Council — on both of which he took a special interest in planning. Ted spoke at public inquiries and was part of the Breckland Research Committee set up in the late 1940s to consider whether, as he put it, 'military and other forms of transgression', including firing ranges, should be allowed on the light-soiled brecks. He wrote in 1948:

> Breckland as we knew it even twenty years ago is vastly changed, and must change ever more quickly with the growth of forests and the new developments in agriculture. But the gain can be considered greater than the loss only up to a certain point; it would be a great impoverishment to thrust the whole of that lovely and interesting country in the jaws of either Mammon or the god of war.

Ted was president of the Norfolk and Norwich Naturalists Society in 1955, and again in 1969 when it celebrated its centenary. He was a past president of the Norfolk Research Committee and a member of its council. He was for many years a member of the council of the Norfolk Naturalists Trust and served on its conservation committee, as a vice-president from 1979–83, and later as a vice-patron. He also served on the council of the London-based British Mycological Society, following Sir Alexander Fleming — the discoverer of penicillin — as a speaker at one meeting.

When one person can claim to have supported so many councils and societies (and the above list is far from complete), it is tempting to ask just how much that person actually does for them — or were these just nominal positions? Not in Ted's case . . . for him membership was always active. In a tribute after his death, Mr Eddie Boosey, chairman of the Norfolk Conservation Corps, told a typical story. The Group had asked him to become their patron when it was founded in 1977. The title 'was meant to be honorary. Ted, however, thought otherwise and has given not only money to help us buy tools but also gave of his time, giving fascinating talks to evening meetings of volunteers, and constant encouragement and praise.'

As a committee man, he was known to be a determined advocate on conservation issues — such as hedgerow management, the erosion of banks on the Broads, pollution of waterways, the uses of chemicals in agriculture, and the need to balance the creeping 'urbanisation' of Norfolk with protection of its natural heritage. In fact, the issues were always, literally, in his view. Ted kept some reminders for himself. Hanging on his wall at home was a group of watercolours depicting idyllic country scenes in the village of Quinton, Worcestershire. And in his library was one especially treasured book containing an eighteenth-century description of Chat Moss, an enchanting stretch of moorland near Manchester; the book had been a present from Arthur Patterson. Referring to these, he once wrote:

> In both cases these rural haunts have been obliterated by the expansion of cities, growing apace under the influence of the industrial revolution. The countryside of East Anglia has not been invaded by bricks and mortar to the same extent but, all the same, in my own lifetime I have seen quite large areas of fields, woods and lanes urbanised.

On the screen his anger rarely showed, but John Mountford recalls: 'One time I saw him almost speechless with anger was in north Norfolk when we found a stretch of sunken lane which should have had hedges on both sides. But a farmer had grubbed out 150 yards of it. Ted managed to say a few words on camera but they did not convey how upset he was.' Ted, however, did indicate his concern for hedgerows more forcibly in his writing . . .

> On a recent visit to the countryside near Colchester, my attention was drawn to a length of roadside hedge, acknowledged by a sympathetic county authority to be worthy of special respect and consideration as a link with the ancient past. Its wealth of native shrubs and trees pointed clearly to its ancestry, well back in medieval times. Scientific studies of England's hedgerows have shown conclusively that the variety of species occurring in them provides a reliable clue to their age and where the mixture is richest they are likely to date from late Saxon or early Norman times, whereas fences planted from the seventeenth century onwards tend to consist dominantly of quickset hawthorn, although some other shrubs and trees may have become established in them here and there.
>
> Sadly, the wholesale clearance of hedges undertaken as a convenience of

Demonstrating the fascination of fungi to youngsters at the Essex Conservation Zone in 1985

modern farming in recent years has involved the destruction of many links with olden days, since little discrimination has been shown by those deciding to amalgamate their fields to facilitate the economic use of multiple ploughs and combine harvesters as a means of attaining greater productivity. While in general one has to accept much of this change, I think that it goes beyond the bounds of civilised action to remove roadside hedges without paying heed to their interest, while in some cases ancient parish boundary hedges merit special consideration and, like special trees, could be protected for the future by means of legally enforceable preservation orders.

As this passage suggests, he was never an enemy of the farmer in general. Ted had a countryman's appreciation of the value of efficient agriculture, and its realistic requirements. It was the individual abuse that he saw as his target . . .

I like to equate the term 'conservation' with care. Its main enemy is narrow expediency, which means advancement in blinkers. Our main concern is the quality of human life as well as its bare survival. We stand at the crossroads where grim prospects can be seen. The more of nature we destroy and pollute, the sooner we shall destroy what makes our own lives worth living.

Along with his lifelong committee work went a rapport with children. There are naturalists who, despairing of the present generation of adults, deliberately concentrate on teaching the young — showing them how to understand and conserve what they still see as wonderful. Ted did so often, but had no need to be consciously an 'educator', for he had an instinctive closeness to children, an eagerness to teach and to learn from them. He made countless visits to schools, regularly showed parties of school-children and teenagers around his land, and served as a school governor in Surlingham. He wrote a weekly newspaper article specifically for the young and in his writing for children always refused to simplify his language to a degree he thought patronising. Often scientific and technical terms were included in his column, and in the regular articles he wrote for *The Bulletin,* a magazine sent to schools in Norfolk. Above all, he always had time for children. Once, in fact, whilst filming in a wood next to a school, he found himself besieged by the pupils who wanted to meet him — one of them bringing a small pet caterpillar to show him. Then and there, Ted stopped the filming and hosted an impromptu half-hour question-and-answer session across the school railings . . . while the BBC's producer hopped from one foot to another, mentally tearing up his schedules!

Perhaps Ted's personal attitude to conservation is best summed up in a beautifully eloquent article he wrote in 1964, entitled 'Let Us Keep Our Sanity':

> 'And this our life, exempt from public haunt,
> Finds tongues in trees, books in the running brooks,
> Sermons in stones and good in everything.
> I would not change it.'

So Shakespeare in *As You Like It* forestalled Gilbert White in presenting the gentle outlook of the country philosopher living close to nature. Now, 400 years after the poet's birth, the English countryside is vastly changed, yet in this thickly populated island miraculously there are still wildernesses 'exempt from public haunt' where 'daisies pied and violets blue, and lady-smocks all silver-white, and cuckoo-buds of yellow hue do paint the meadows with delight' and great free spaces where 'the lark at heaven's gate sings'.

Here in East Anglia we have largely escaped the stranglehold of industrial expansion and the sprawling overgrowth of cities. But we have been reminded recently of what professional planners have in mind for the future: a more even distribution of industry, homes and people over the length and breadth of the land until ultimately it will become impossible to find a secluded wilderness. No place will be 'exempt from public haunt'. With this threat in the offing I make no apology for standing out against it for what I believe to be the ultimate good.

I am very jealous for the pastoral peace of the East Anglian countryside. If it is destroyed, where will town dwellers and all the sick-of-suburbs people turn to find unspoiled country? Let us remain a breathing space for the cure of souls, rejoicing in honest agriculture, forestry and the like and cherishing the serene beauty of our Broads and coast. I am sure we can still do this and live.

9 🙪 Putting pen to paper

Start writing, and what is in your mind will flow out with the ink like a spring out of the ground; be sparing with adjectives and keep something in the locker for another time.

hat was the invaluable advice Ted received from Arthur Patterson during those long, winter evenings at Ibis Lodge. The old man had been writing for newspapers since the 1880s and influenced Ted in his journalism as in so much else. Every day for forty years something did come 'out of the locker' — poetic, informative, whimsical. Ted never repeated himself, was never dull . . . and many wondered how he kept it up. The answer, in part, is that he found his mentor's words — 'Don't think it out; if anything is there it will come out as you put pen to paper' — were strangely true. If he started, words came. They were the fruit, of course, of his ceaseless, teeming observations. But he sometimes felt there was magic at work, too. . .

I gather my subject out of the air, out of the experience. Sometimes a letter triggers it off. But quite often I just look out of the window for inspiration or take a breath of fresh air outside the back door, and I see something! And there I have the nucleus of an article. There are occasions when I have to race against time and it comes out like fury. It just pours out because I have insisted on my subconscious giving me something — and it happens!

That facility was shaped by a lifetime of reading — from those early childhood bedside tales, and the *Boys' Own* comic jottings of 'Nat the Naturalist', right through to the classic works of literature. Early encouragement by his headmaster helped him enormously, as did a correspondence course in literature which he undertook after he left school. As he grew up, there was a long list of favourite authors in Ted's life. When he was twelve it was the graphic world of Charles Dickens; in adolescence, he devoured books by the late-Victorian traveller W. H. Hudson (*The Naturalist in Patagonia* and others). His correspondence course introduced him to early writers like Addison, Cranmer and Charles Lamb. And he shared with Patterson a love of America's Henry Thoreau, Walter Scott, Daniel Defoe and the language of the King James Bible. In later years he declared in a radio interview:

> I aim at being lucid, because the greatest communicator that I know in my field is, of course, Gerald Durrell — author of *My Family and Other Animals* — because he has that sense of humour, and I always keep that going as well, not a nonsense humour, but there are some very curious incidents and there are opportunities for humour.

It was on Durrell's style of writing and presentation that he hoped to model his own autobiography. Of Cranmer and Lamb, he said:

> I absorbed a feeling . . . and that comes into the construction of my writing. So one owes one's developing style to many in the past.

The result sometimes reads like poetry, as in this piece which appeared in *The Guardian:*

> Sunrise over the fen on these autumn mornings brings transient splendour to a realm of dew-wet reeds and a lingering cloak of mist. Through a haze of rose which turns to gold, countless geometric webs of spiders bridge darkling gaps, glittering and opalescent. Spear-leaves and drooping purple reed-plumes are beaded with silver and the pin-cushion umbels of angelica are pricked out with a million diamond points of light.
>
> Tassels of hemp agrimony and magenta spires of loosestrife achieve a brightness and perfection which beautifies them, while white bellbines shine with the pallor of fading stars through the morning vapours. There is a scent of water mint distilled from the night. The air is so still that even the gossamer does not tremble. The reed-warblers have gone: there is no chorus of chattering and husky music to greet the new day; but presently a wren trills, a woodpecker's 'chipping' breaks the silence of the nearby woods and bullfinches utter plaintive whistles in the sallow bushes.
>
> A pheasant wakes in a sedgy jungle roost and rises like a rocket, scattering the dew in its rude progress and raising a general alarm. The sun's warmth now begins to be felt. Soon bumble-bees are astir; wasps begin their hunting and the first dragonfly wakes with a rustle and fret of wings. The mist and its magic have evaporated: the sparkling webs have dried to near invisibility and only the recesses of the lush undergrowth are still wet. The fen is set fair for a golden day as the peacock and brimstone butterflies come swooping out to the flowers.

He told a journalist in 1986:

> If I have a principle, I like to go for the 'actuality' of a happening. People see the beginning, and it's often a mystery, and I try to solve it in the course of the article. I convey this news straight into my writing; it gives it a freshness and keeps me enthusiastic. That's the spirit of the thing. I seek adventures and I write them up in a form which I hope will be understandable to the greatest number of people.

Ted, a man to whom words like 'cryptogamous' and 'sporangium' came

At his desk, out on the fen, or a small insect carried to him by a child — any observation could inspire Ted's vivid, often spontaneous, prose

easily, nonetheless was always conscious of the need to write, like Defoe, in plain English . . .

> Science, of course, is a cult of exactitude, and we must honour science for that. But it tends to obscure things for so many people by the wording it uses. If you are a scientist with a free spirit, you want to share your excitement and make people envisage it in a way which they can understand, using ordinary language.

So for forty years he conducted his *EDP* column like a dialogue — asking questions, reporting answers he had received from others, basing many of his articles on what readers told him. With his natural wish to communicate, he never regarded his broadcasting or journalism as less important than his research . . .

> I write for the pleasure of what I imagine to be a great circle of friends and, although occasionally taking up the cudgel where environmental threat arises, I seek to awaken consciences in high places through gentle pointers. Used sparingly, this policy has often proved effective.

131

In his writing, as in his science, Ted tried to preserve something of the late-Victorian manner. An obituary he wrote for old friend and fellow *EDP* writer Eric Fowler — 'Jonathan Mardle' — reveals his own tastes:

> His style, *belle lettre* in character, savouring that of some great essayists of the eighteenth and nineteenth centuries — such as Addison and whimsical Charles Lamb — kept alive sweetening influences from the past, while disciplining them discerningly from the long-winded tendencies of Victorian journalism which predominated in the Press until it was succeeded by the mindless concentration on 'shock' headlines, 'hard news', violence, misery and scandal that now characterises much of the National Press and, increasingly, radio, television and even our provincial newspapers. This revolution, reducing standards below mediocrity, partly caused by advancing technology and its economic advantages, has become overmuch concerned with depressing news, while less space is given than formerly to the gentler but very meaningful topics featured in the past.

When, in 1982, Ted put together a selection of his writings with illustrations by David Poole (*Countryside Reflections,* published by Wilson-Poole), he said he had deliberately focused on his more poetic writings — those with more 'emotion' in them.

Ted, then, was always conscious of *how* he wrote, as well as *what* he wrote. Nowhere was that more important to him than in his frequent writings for children. He deliberately refused to over-simplify his language for them, believing that children who are interested enough will make an effort to understand, and that some writing aimed at children suffers from being too patronising. This piece from *The Bulletin,* a newsletter sent to Norfolk schools, was one of a regular series of nature articles by Ted later republished as a short book, entitled *For Your Delight*:

WATER INSECTS

> Insects which live in ponds and ditches include many which spend only their larval life in water while the adults emerge and take wing, enjoying the freedom of the air. Examples are mayflies, dragonflies and caddis flies. There are others which spend their whole lives in or on water and these include all water beetles and water bugs; but these insects are in nearly all cases equipped with wings so that they can travel from one pond to another when the need arises, or, as happens at certain seasons, when they feel the urge to migrate. Shallow ponds tend to dry up in summer and their insects have to seek new homes. Overcrowding can be another cause of mass exodus for the particular species involved. However, exploratory flights are also made from time to time simply as a means of colonising all available pieces of water and providing the fullest opportunities for increasing the range of the insects.

10 ❧ A freelance takes wing

ed had never been well paid. In 1956, when he left the museum, he had just received a rise and the job was worth £44 a month. Writing was earning him another £28 a month. He had decided to resign from his job believing that the extra time could be used to make more money from writing. When it became a reality, however, his first reaction to freedom was to feel lost. There were months, Phyllis recalls, when he did little but write his daily articles and go for walks on the fen. Released from the framework of his museum duties, it seems he needed time to adjust. Gradually, though, he began to spread his wings — writing and undertaking more broadcasting. He also found a new post — for even less money: the Norfolk Naturalists Trust were in trouble, having lost their secretary, and asked him to stand in temporarily on part-time pay. But he soon found that the job demanded his full-time attention and, based in offices at the Assembly House in Norwich, he stayed from 1959 to 1963 — often sharing his desk, after school hours, with his daughters. Even there he enjoyed nature's revelations . . .

> This morning, I was a little surprised to see a common field slug *(Agriolimax reticulatus)* crawling in the middle of the Assembly House car park.

Alice, Ted's mother, had come to live with them. His father, Jimmy, had died in February 1949 after years of being virtually an invalid with tuberculosis, and the old lady, no longer well, now lived at Wheatfen, where she remained until her death in 1958 aged eighty-six.

It was in 1960 that the Ellises finally bought their house — though they still could not afford the asking price of under £5,000. Phyllis, who had been left a bungalow in a will, was able to contribute just over half. For the rest, friends gave them a private mortgage. Enough money was kept back from the house purchase to enable them to buy their first new — and first reliable — car, a Morris Oxford van. They had to manage (until 1966) without mains electricity, though, relying for a time on an old, second-hand generator — installed by Phyllis's uncle Frank — which chugged away in the engine house, sometimes powering a saw by belt drive and sometimes hitched up to a few feeble light bulbs. Running on agricultural diesel oil, it took a hefty handle to start it, noisily. Ted recalled one morning when . . .

There was an immediate panic among the grasshoppers near the source of the noise and vibration and I was interested to see that the insects leapt away in a great hurry, spreading out fan-wise and continuing for ten yards or so before they showed any signs of settling down.

When that temperamental machine finally broke down they went back to paraffin lamps and discovered that the brilliant white light of a Tilley lamp does something an electric bulb does not: it imitates the signals of female glow-worms — and courting males, who were not fooled by electric light bulbs, flocked to them.

In that same year of 1960 — it was one that saw many changes — they decided to foster Robert Bailey — always known as Willy — who was then a twelve-year-old living in an orphanage. In a sense, Willy was one of dozens. Countless children stayed at Wheatfen for weeks or months if their families were in trouble, or a parent was in hospital. Others, keen on natural history, were encouraged to regard Wheatfen as a second home, gaining regular guidance and encouragement from Ted. But Willy came to have a special place in the family; he stayed whenever he was home from boarding school and continued to return home there after he joined the army when he was sixteen, always regarding Ted and Phyllis as his mum and dad. Later, they were to encourage the development of his talents as a musical instrument maker.

The family's fortunes were slowly getting better, and so were those of the area as well when, in 1963, improvements at the Whitlingham sewage works began to encourage a return of many declining species to Ted's home fens. Again, he watched and recorded the changes carefully . . .

Although detergent foam still accumulates in the river at Whitlingham sewage outfall at times, recent improvements carried out at the works there and in Norwich generally have gone a long way towards cleaning up the Yare. The fishing has improved very noticeably in the last two seasons and the fish have looked healthier. One sign of recovery has been the return of the stickle-backs, which all but vanished when the river was in a poor state. In 1963, eels turned up in the Yare broads in phenomenal numbers and a great many are still there wintering in the mud, so that it has been found worthwhile to go after them with eelpicks again.

Rockland Broad used to be a great place for pike in the old days until the river became polluted. Now, after a long interval, these have reappeared in fair numbers. At the moment, there are plenty of freshwater shrimps in these waters, together with smaller crustaceans and much microscopic plant life, all providing sustenance for the fish.

However, there is nothing like the former rich variety and abundance of aquatic snails and insects known in this Broad when water weeds flourished. I rather doubt whether these will return to their former glory because there are still substances harmful to them in the water.

In her final years, Alice, Ted's mother, lived with the family at Wheatfen. Here she is pictured at eighty-three, still creating her fine embroidered landscapes

A major addition to Ted's journalism came, in January 1964 when *The Guardian* asked him to join the team of regular contributors to its 'Country Diary'. From then on he wrote a regular fortnightly article on Norfolk and Suffolk. The work introduced him to many new friends among the column's regular writers. One of them was W. D. Campbell who, writing in the paper after Ted's death, recalled '. . . his ability when we came across such comparative rarities as a bee hawk moth or the greater broomrape, to quote the year of the last known record. But my outstanding memory of the typical Ted is of the time when, on meeting him by chance in London one morning, he greeted me with: "Hello, Bill, I've just had a new experience. I have often been bitten by a six-spot ladybird, but this morning, for the first time ever, I had a nip from a two-spot!"'

A more serious accident happened in October 1964 causing casualties among his plentiful household bugs, spiders, slugs and pets. Fire broke out at Wheatfen in the early hours of the morning. It started in the kitchen, in a box containing old newspapers, and the Ellises, asleep upstairs, woke to a house full of smoke. They were in time to tackle the blaze successfully with buckets of well water but, as the humans got their breath back, Ted saw two harvest mice 'apparently lifeless lying huddled together on the leafy floor of their cage like babes in the wood.' Still in his pyjamas, he carefully carried them outside for air and was relieved to see them recover in time for breakfast. The blackened walls and furniture took weeks to clean.

In 1965, the biggest writing project of Ted's career was published — a long-awaited, definitive volume, *The Broads*. He edited the four hundred-page book, wrote six of its fifteen chapters entirely (plus two lengthy appendices), and jointly wrote three other chapters with specialist contributors,

Rescued! This lovable pair of harvest mice escaped a serious blaze at Ted's home when the naturalist succeeded in reviving them

covering every aspect of Broadland natural history. The book, published in the Collins 'New Naturalist' series, has since become a standard work, and Ted saw it as one of the highlights of his career. But he hated writing it! It was a piece of work which had virtually watched its contributors grow old in the making. The book took Ted seventeen years to complete — so long that the publishers lost their original colour plates and had to make do with black-and-white photographs. For years, letters of increasing desperation came, asking Ted when it would be ready. The delay had already been a sore point between Ted and his old curator way back in 1956. (Roy Rainbird Clarke was one of the contributors.)

'It was always very difficult to get him to settle down unless he had a firm deadline to meet,' Phyllis says. 'It was much better — though I couldn't make the publishers realise it — to say to Ted: "We must have chapter one by 3 December at the very latest", than to say "We want the whole book finished some time next year." He could work to a time, but you had to give him a time — and split things up so there was not too much to do before that time.' It is true that one delay was the need to wait for Dr Lambert to complete her research on the origins of the Broads. But, from the early 1960s, she was one of those writing him good-natured letters . . . urging him to 'lock yourself away and get it finished.'

Ted never took on another full-length book, though he was approached with a number of offers, including some which would have been well paid and some which would have made intelligent use of his knowledge. He always claimed he was too busy; as the 'busy-ness' sometimes involved opening fetes and attending annual dinners, however, the truth seems to be more that he did not relish the long, slow business of definitive authorship. Spontaneity and observation, immediately recorded, were his forte. The mid-1960s found him always busy, however. He still wrote regularly for *The Sunday Companion,* wrote and illustrated articles for a fishing magazine and, above all, these were the broadcasting years.

He had done occasional radio work since 1946, and had featured in nationally-networked broadcasts on the old Home Service, enjoying a regular slot touring the country as part of a specialist team which produced a programme on the natural history of different localities. His work increased when the BBC came to Norwich to set up the Midland regional service. As well as making increasingly frequent appearances 'on the air', he also rapidly became established as the Corporation's regional consultant on nature topics. Ted's expertise always lay behind far more programmes than used his face or voice.

The television programme 'Look East' and its forerunner 'East at 6.10' had given him regular work and, in 1964, he also became resident naturalist for the BBC's monthly 'On Camera: In the Country'; which was produced by Gordon Moseley and also featured David Richardson, the farmer/ broadcaster. Again from 1964, and running until 1970, his fifteen-minute 'Nature Postbag' on BBC Radio 4 Midland is estimated — at one time — to have had a million listeners. There were many one-off broadcasts, including appearances in 'Woman's Hour' on the old Light Programme, and sometimes on Radio 4. Off the air, Ted became a natural history consultant for television, assisting with programmes such as the nationally-networked 'Nature Trail' in the mid 1960s.

Then, in April 1980, he was invited to take part in a new regional television magazine series 'Weekend', produced by Brian Fawcett, and his face as well as his voice became famous. With John Mountford as presenter, it became one of the most popular television programmes in the country. In the early 1980s Ted's regular audience was estimated at half-a-million, then a record-breaking figure for BBC Norwich. It was through this series that the public came to link Ted and John Mountford together, as they travelled far and wide in an informative, often humorous nature 'double act'. Appearances on 'Look East' continued whenever Ted could contribute to its more topical, newsy format, often as a spokesman on conservation issues; and he could also be seen in a nature postbag slot on the monthly 'Out of Town' programme.

The colour photographs which so often flashed up behind Ted on the screen — an orchid or a natterjack toad, a giant hogweed or a heron — were usually taken by him, too. Within the broadcasting world, they were regarded as another of the marvels of the Ted Ellis story, for until he was in his late fifties, Ted had never handled anything more sophisticated than a Brownie box camera. The sudden development of this skill astounded hardened BBC technical staff, who were quick to recognise a professional standard in a man who had never had a lesson. It seems he did it simply by instinct. Ted rarely took more than one shot; he got it right first time — a rare feat, even for a professional — and seemed to have a natural eye for photographic composition. Typically, though, the technical side never interested him . . . and he always sent his films to the chemist for processing.

How did Ted become a photographer? John, his son, on leave from a navy posting in the West Indies, was responsible. He took some slides at Wheatfen and they aroused Ted's curiosity. When John's leave ended he left his father with a Pentax single lens reflex camera and basic instructions. Ted's enthusiasm stemmed from his realisation of the way photography could aid observation, and how it could reduce the need to collect specimens. He eventually assembled a collection of an estimated 18,000 slides — every one taken by him, all of which were carefully labelled, indexed and arranged in a visual 'library' at his home. Of course, his talks were then illustrated with the slides, and his audiences quickly appreciated that he had brought his poetry to this new medium, too, with shots of ice-crystals on a pool, or frost on a cobweb. His photographs were also used in a series of natural history colour guides which he wrote for Jarrold Colour Publications in the 1970s, and in a series of calendars that they produced.

It wasn't just photographic slides that Ted took to the BBC studios, however. He often turned up with his own scenery — arriving in his battered car crammed with boxes of reeds, bushes, grass and plants, and staggering into the studio like a walking fen, invisible behind his paraphernalia, to spend several happy hours arranging his habitat to perfection before he popped out on the air. Complicated though his set-ups were, he rarely forgot to bring anything that he might need for the broadcast — except on one occasion . . . his false teeth!

As he staggered into the studio no-one was more relieved to see him than the receptionists. For it wasn't only letters that arrived in Ted's nature postbags. His audiences also sent him matchboxes with beetles in them, strange parcels that rustled if you put your ear close to them, pieces of damp wood, jam jars of ants, spiders of every shape, size and colour, decaying pieces of vegetation — not to mention fish, fungi, frogs, feathers and fossils. '. . . And the trouble was', said John Mountford, 'Ted only came in once a week! That meant the poor receptionists had to live with some of these things for quite some time. But however disgusting the contents of a little parcel looked, Ted always greeted each one with relish.'

Often, when he went to the Norwich studios to do a broadcast — now a nationally recognised personality — he would also go back to share some of those surprises that had come through the mail with staff at his old work-place, the Castle Museum — arriving rather like a modest elder statesman. 'We would all gather round, I suppose a bit like dogs welcoming the master home!' says Dr Tony Irwin, the Castle's present Keeper of Natural History. 'He had given so much of his life to the place, and I think it was some recompense to him to find us welcoming and interested, and carrying on his work.'

In August 1982, Ted was awarded the Royal Television Society's regional award for his contribution to television over twenty years.

It was in another field, however, that he gained the award which stood out as a great highlight of his life. It came in 1970 — fittingly, European Conservation Year — when three separate departments at the Norwich-based University of East Anglia, which had been founded during the peak years of his career, unexpectedly recommended him for an honorary doctorate. That triple nomination marked, finally, the academic recognition which scientists had privately given him for years. Ted, who had left elementary school at fifteen, without an examination success to his name, became . . . Doctor E. A. Ellis. As one might expect, he rarely used the title but he regarded the honour as a climax in his career and was much moved by the acceptance it implied.

'In an age of specialisation, he is an invaluable link-man between disciplines, and no small part of his unique knowledge has found its origins in his minutely detailed daily observations . . .' said the Public Orator as Ted, for once without the familiar duffle-coat and gum boots, stood on the stage looking about him with an air of modest authority dressed, in the colourful cap and gown of academia, as brightly as in those boyhood red sweaters. Phyllis recalls: 'He didn't feel proud. He was never proud of anything. He was a simple character. But he did feel honoured.' As he heard himself described as 'last of the old school of self-taught and multi-disciplined field naturalists', perhaps many faces from the past flashed before him. And perhaps the thought . . . what a cartoon Patterson would have made of it!

Although his own efforts had earned him that place among scholars, Ted had remained in awe of the university world, regarding it as a magical place from which he had been excluded. Sometimes he would say he had been taught, in his own way, by nature. Yet, when the time came, it was important to him for his own eldest daughter, Mary, to go to university. (She did — and gained a degree in French.)

As if in recognition of both sides of his achievement — as a communicator and a naturalist — Ted was honoured in a different way, also in 1970, when he was asked to write the 'Meditations' for a special conservation service in Norwich Cathedral. Mindful of those early Lessons he had heard as a choirboy, he wrote:

> We give thanks, oh God, for the gift of Life on this earth: for all life. Thy mysteries surround us, in the depths of Space and the eternity of Time. The sunshine and the rainbow delight our eyes. In the peace of a starry night and in the shadow of the mountain we are aware of Thy presence. Our senses are comforted by the sweet distillations of flowers; our hearts are warmed by kinship with Man and Nature. Cold and heat, storm and calm, darkness and light, diversify our pilgrimage. Our spirits ebb and flow like the tides of the ocean and waves upon the shore; but to our consciousness of elemental things is added, in Mankind, a spirit of reflection and forethought, whereby we have gained stewardship of this world of ancient wealth and living wonder.
>
> As we pause to consider our involvement in the destiny of this glorious inheritance, let us resolve that our works henceforth may be attuned to the music that springs from our hearts in thankfulness for Thy great mercies.
>
> In our selfishness and arrogance we have betrayed Thy trust. In our demands for luxury we have neglected the starving, wasted Thy gifts and sullied the pure air, the rivers and the seas. As we gather to ourselves the bounty of the earth, we weigh not the consequences. We isolate ourselves in pride and defiance of Thy perfect Law. We molest our fellow men and destroy

the Eden of Thy creation as locusts lay waste a green land.

All of us who are gathered in this sanctuary are to some extent aware of our collective failure to honour the code of life which Thou hast set before us. We pray that we may reject what is evil and that we may discipline our actions henceforth to the furtherance of Thy design, with humility, understanding and compassion.

These were years of recognition in many ways. Ted was honoured with the Queen's Silver Jubilee Medal in 1977. In 1976, he was even registered for VAT, when his turnover that year exceeded £7,500. (Not surprisingly though, when the threshold figure rose to £15,000 in 1982, Phyllis was relieved of the task of keeping VAT books again!) None of these many honours, however, had a subduing effect on Ted's approach to his work; and, even though his years were advancing and his wisdom increasing, he still showed all the enthusiasm of boyhood . . .

Yesterday with three fellow naturalists, I enjoyed the hospitality of a shrimper friend on one of his regular working trips out of Yarmouth. Chugging away northwards from Gorleston harbour on the afternoon ebb, with enough breeze to enliven the grey anonymous waters, we made for a point off Caister before pausing to lower the trawl nets. Then, wallowing in the swell with the trawls scraping a relatively hard bottom, we awaited our first glimpse of treasure from the deep and at the same time were initiated into the art of discerning sea bed contours by noting subtle changes in wave action.

In the first haul, consisting mainly of pink shrimps (Aesop's prawns), we were confronted with swarms of little goggle-eyed iridescent squids which squirted ink over everything and nipped us with their parrot-like beaks when we handled them. There were small common starfish, larger sun stars, various sea slugs, with elegant crests on their backs, glassy sea gooseberries, slippery butterfish, dragonets, bearded and armour-plated pogges, small sponges, oaten-pipes, corallines with rose-pink tentacles, yellow many-jointed sea spiders *(Pycnogonum littorale),* shore crabs, swimming crabs and an occasional little spider crab and fingered translucent fronds of the gelatinous organism notorious for producing the 'Dogger Bank Itch'.

The catch of shrimps was not up to expectations so several more hauls were made during the rest of the tide, including one which took all hands to lift when the 'catch' consisted of a mass of a reddish sandy concretion from the sea bed.

Our host's toil brought us some very pleasant rewards from time to time, including a single specimen of the rare little chocolate-banded shrimp *(Philocheras fasciatus),* transparent prawns, with green egg masses *(Processa edulis),* and a weird crustacean with long antennae and a scorpion's tail *(Astacilla longicornis),* all of which have now been added to the zoological treasures of the Norfolk Room in Norwich Castle Museum, together with a piece of amber which came up with the shrimps.

Perhaps nothing illustrates his enthusiasm better than the story of some fieldwork he undertook during a return visit to Guernsey in 1979. His naturalist friend Tim Peet, who lives on the island, recalls: 'During a spring visit to Guernsey, local naturalists asked him to do a plant survey in one of our precious orchid meadows. At five in the morning, we were awoken by groans from the living room, to find Ted in his pyjamas lying on the floor with acute sciatica. His back happily quickly recovered but he found walking uncomfortable. He was not to be put off doing the botanical survey, however, and discovered that the best position for looking at the plants was on all fours. So, on a bright May afternoon Ted crawled through this wet Guernsey meadow, notebook in one hand, camera round his waist, happily recording the plants. The sight was exactly that of the layman's vision of an eccentric botanist! What an enthusiast!'

In these years of fame, Ted found himself called upon to fill more and more public engagements. There was a conflict, in fact, between his wish to do scientific work and his willingness to do anything for anybody. As he became a local personality, more and more of the invitations had less and less to do with natural history. 'He spent a lot of time,' says Phyllis, 'writing letters or answering the phone.' She might have added . . . or opening fetes, guesting at annual dinners, launching scouts regattas, and judging poetry competitions. All these, and more, became part of life. In many ways he enjoyed it, and welcomed the chance to represent natural history in different places. He also enjoyed being a recognised part of the community, and felt some obligation to the public for his popularity. But he regretted not having enough time for research.

One of his stranger honours — though one that he enjoyed, appealing as it did to his love of Norfolk culture — came when he was made an honorary member of the Kemp's Men morris dancing side. Though he never actually danced with them, he did lead them through the streets of Norwich, dressed in the costume of a Whiffler (a traditional servant of the Lord Mayor), during celebrations to mark the anniversary of Will Kemp's historic nine-days' dance from London to Norwich. In fact, it was not the first time he had been a Whiffler. He donned the colourful garb for a procession in Norwich round about 1930, in which Norfolk's traditional Snap appeared. What's more, he wrote a special song for the celebration:

> The Mayor of Norwich and his train is comin' down o' Cockey Lane;
> Here come the Whifflers runnin' quick to knock ye down with a bit o' stick.

> CHORUS

> Make way for Snap! Look out!
> Old Snap's a one for blasting with his fiery breath
> All them that stop to taste o' death!
> So mind the way! Mind the way!

Late recognition — Ted became known to thousands through BBC broadcasts and in 1970 *(below left)* he donned academic gown to receive an honorary doctorate
Below right: Ted took on many roles in the community — here seen in fine plumage leading Morris dancers through Norwich as a traditional 'Whiffler'

Snap is as savage as Hell today:
Savage as the Devil let loose, I say!
Snap, snap! Snap, snap! Snap go his jaws on this and that!

Blow me! Old Snap ha' just seen red: a silly young fule ha' lost his head!
An' that 'on't stay his appetite: he'll catch another dozen afore tonight!

The Mayor ha' got a ruddy face: I shouldn't wonder if he lace
His lemonade wi' dragon's blood: that must be somethin' werry good!

Now if too many Mayors think that dragon's blood is good to drink,
Poor Snap'll go right off his food an' slowly die o' lassitude.

But Snap might one day change his fare an' acquire a taste for a Norwich Mayor.
I think that's a change we'd like to see, for it might give a chance to you and me!

It poured in torrents that day, and the dye in the Whiffler's red hat ran right down the back of Ted's coat!

He was also giving more and more talks and lectures in these years — to small groups as well as large, one night filling a lecture theatre at the university and another standing up in a draughty village hall. He never charged a fee and until the cost of travel became too much, would not even take expenses. When societies insisted on giving a fee, he would ask them to donate it to charity. For years he was out at least once, and often several nights a week. As he grew older, Phyllis would drive him to and from engagements. In one year alone they worked out that he had had to turn down 270 requests to talk!

Ted enjoyed his flair for pitching a speech at a level to suit any audience — young or old, experts or novices. It is telling that when he wrote a tribute to his old friend Henry Howard, who had died in 1957, Ted emphasised the fact that . . .

> With equal facility he could coach a pupil . . . discourse on the beauties of shell life to a Women's Institute, deliver a profound lecture to a scientific society or delight children with illustrated accounts of his travels.

He enjoyed meeting Norfolk country people — fascinated by the dialect and speaking it fluently — but was equally at home when, one evening, looking back down the room, he could see the Queen sitting to one side of his projector, and the Queen Mother on the other! The occasion was a Women's Institute meeting at a Norfolk village hall, where the Queen Mother was President, usually attending a meeting once a year. Minutes before she arrived, Ted's box of slides went crashing onto the floor and spilled everywhere. But, says Phyllis, 'Fortunately, for what must have been the first time in his life, he had made a list of the order he was going to show them in.' So as the Royal party arrived, and everyone rose to sing the National Anthem, there was Ted struggling to fit little plastic squares into

A royal occasion — Ted has to improvise when he discovers he is to be the Queen's guide

little plastic slots, the sound of his cursing mercifully drowned by the piano! But all went well and, it is said, the Queen Mother, a keen amateur naturalist, asked questions about every slide as it came onto the screen — there were over a hundred!

Ted met the Queen again at the opening of the Ranworth Broad nature centre . . . and again there were mishaps. As he stood on the bridge, shivering in the wind, beside David Attenborough, he heard there would be a slight delay — someone had forgotten to bring gumboots for the Queen. When she did arrive, Ted got a shock, as he was told — 'By the way, you're showing her round!' Though unprepared, he soon got into his stride, and the photographs show him wandering around Ranworth, hands in his pockets as usual, peering into odd corners and enthusing merrily while the Queen walked beside him.

Phyllis did a great deal, over the years, to try to protect Ted from too many demands, and from the danger of exploitation that his willingness and disregard for money made him prey to. Any story of Ted's life is, more than is often realised, also her story. She was, as one friend put it, 'always in the background, but never under his shadow'. The Reverend Sir Alan Webster praised her in 1986 for her 'heroic hospitality and ability to give care and support over many years in a way of life where the public could make daunting demands on what was private,' and perceptively observed that 'regularity of work required from a naturalist who earned his own living could only be achieved by the encouragement, wisdom and steadfastness which comes from a supportive home.'

Phyllis hassled him to meet work deadlines, brought the children up, catered for endless guests, nursed him, cycled three miles to school each day to help support the family, did as much of the physical work around Wheatfen as Russell . . . and brewed the famous Wheatfen beer, the effects of which could be devastating. At one party for unsuspecting BBC staff, guests are said to have staggered into the ditches and dykes on the way home and, in some cases, slept there. Another guest who thought he could drive home thought again after a few hundred yards, and was found in the morning, asleep, just around the corner.

Most of the phone calls were screened by Phyllis, answering queries herself if possible, or calling on Russell for the answers. 'Ted didn't like it, but he wouldn't have got anything done otherwise.' She tried to bring commonsense to the endless public engagements — 'at least I drew the line at fancy dress competitions!' — and she sometimes acted, secretly, as an agent: calling up people who had promised him money, organising contracts or asking for rises on his behalf. That, too, was something he never knew. Ted would never ask for a rise, chase a debtor or set a price for his work. Intensely trusting and loyal himself, he stuck by the principle 'People will give me what they think I am worth.' Despite his popularity, he sometimes expressed a fear that if he asked for too much — 'People will not want me.' He never had an official agent, therefore, and was strongly opposed to the idea. It seemed to go against his nature to push himself. Sometimes the self-employed have to. 'I think people always assume we were well off because they saw him on TV,' says Phyllis; but that was not the case — they made ends meet, as much through Phyllis's efforts as those of Ted himself.

At the height of Ted's public fame in 1982, when he had become a household name, blindness threatened him. The man who lived by observation suffered a detached retina and, for days, did nothing about it. Not realising the seriousness of the strange purplish tint to his vision, which developed whilst on holiday in Devon, he refused to see a doctor. But on his return, he did — and was rushed into hospital for an emergency operation. Forced to lie still in bed, it was the only fortnight in forty years that he completely stopped writing and broadcasting. His sight was saved, but it had been close, and he was not able to drive for a year afterwards.

Then, in 1983, tragedy struck the Wheatfen partnership when one of its members was lost. Russell, Phyllis and Ted had supported and depended on each other in so many ways for half a lifetime, but on the Friday before Christmas 1983 Russell Sewell, now white-haired and as old as the century, died in hospital. John, Ted's eldest son, sat beside him singing *Speed, Bonnie Boat,* the favourite tune that Russell often whistled as he worked on his garden. He had been with them for thirty-seven years, and Ted was deeply shaken.

As the Wheatfen house slowly adjusted to the absence of that quiet man, who used to sit in his chair reading encyclopaedias of an evening, another blow came. In July 1985, quite unexpectedly, the BBC dropped Ted and a number of other regular contributors, seemingly in pursuit of a new image. Ted took it personally, and was both shocked and hurt. 'He said that when they told him, his stomach dropped,' Phyllis recalls. Repeatedly, when talking to friends, he returned to the same question: Why, when he was still receiving dozens of letters a day, should the BBC not want him? As in the museum years, it had seemed that Ted had become an institution. But the answer has more to do with general policy than personalities; the BBC had decided to shift the emphasis towards news and investigative reporting — slots into which Ted did not easily fit.

Behind Ted's confusion must have lain the knowledge that, consistent with his lifelong principles, he had been intensely loyal to the BBC, repeatedly turning down better-paid offers from commercial television and even, when Anglia TV wanted to make a film about him, *A Man For All Seasons,* first asking his usual employers if they minded. The letters kept coming, and he kept answering them but, privately, he went into a period of depression, rousing himself only when visitors arrived. He did, however, make his first video in 1985 with John Mountford who was now running a private studio. It was called *Ted Ellis — A Limited Edition.*

John recalls one filming session with Ted when the conversation turned to thoughts of what tomorrow might bring: 'I said to him: "Are you fearful for the future?" Instead of thinking about himself, he thought of his home and said: "I wouldn't like Wheatfen to go to someone who would spoil it by 'gardening' — by tidying it up too much. I hope it will go to someone who will look after it by not looking after it, as I have done." I realised that the words were likely to be his epitaph, and I felt that he knew that too.' Perhaps Ted was again thinking of his own hopes when, in October 1985, he wrote in the *EDP* of a ceremony he had attended to mark the fiftieth anniversary of Arthur Patterson's death:

I felt that John Knowlittle would have been happy to have thought there had been avocet seen on Breydon yesterday and that his favourite wilderness of creeks and mudflats was still cherished for its freedom and living wonders by caring people so long after his departure from the scene.

In 1986, Ted became ill and, again, would not see a doctor. In May, at a Norfolk Naturalists Trust open day at Cley, he was still guiding visitors. But the families who took walks with him never guessed that he was, by then, on a diet of bread and warm milk, which Phyllis brought in a vacuum flask. 'He walked up and down the shingle bank twice, showing things to people,' says Phyllis. 'I had to stop him going a third time!' It was his last major public appearance.

Ted was taken into hospital on 12 June 1986 and underwent a stomach operation on the morning of Sunday 15 June. He refused pain-killers whilst in hospital, saying they 'numb the mind'. The *EDP* kept his series going by reprinting old articles, and friends smuggled specimens into the hospital to cheer him up. The Reverend Kit Chalcraft, a former Surlingham vicar and family friend, also visited, and was struck by the lack of embarrassment in Ted's first words — 'Oh . . . have you come about the funeral?' Ted added, 'They have put me in the same bed,' pointing out the irony that he was in the bed where Russell had died nearly three years previously. Repeatedly, he told visitors that he wanted a simple, village funeral . . . 'like Russell's'.

It was at that time that he composed a piece of writing which stands out in the memory of his friends. His fortnightly *Guardian* article was due and Ted, very weak and lying in a small, bare side-room, could see nothing but a patch of sky through one high window. There was little of nature around him. And so he began . . .

> For the past week, my view of Norfolk has been restricted to what can be seen from a hospital bed in Norwich. Mostly, I have had to be content with the sky itself, in whose heights vapours have assumed formations resembling the planks of Noah's Arks, or curdled foam in a bath tub. At times, jet aircraft have suddenly betrayed their far-off presence, seeming to climb like snakes on invisible ladders, their bright trails soon dissolving and giving birth to new and fantastic cloud structures.
>
> In this floating kingdom where one expects a magic carpet to glide by at any moment, and the gold of cornfields is diffused in drifting wraiths against the sky's azure ceiling, I have glimpsed swifts arrowing darkly and minutely at the limit of visibility.

With typical understatement, he said later: 'After I had written that, I felt rather tired'.

During those days, as he lay in bed, Ted's mind returned often to work he had not completed — or to the autobiography he hoped to write. 'There will be magic on every page,' he told his daughter Mary, 'For I am a magical man!' He began jotting notes, in his tiny precise writing, on scraps of paper — brief, cryptic reminders to himself like 'the story of the adjutant stork and the porcupine' . . . or 'my pet missel-thrush'. One note suggests that the first chapter be called 'From Guernsey With Love'.

When friends visited the hospital he dwelt often on the early years — sunlight over the Guernsey cliffs, early morning walks by Breydon . . . 'The great silver water beetles! I remember when Harry, old Rumbelow and I were caught by the police!' he told Tony Irwin. The trio, walking near the Yarmouth railway track, were carrying pond nets. To a wartime train passenger flashing by, they looked like rifles. By the time the story reached Yarmouth police, they *were* rifles. And by the time the police tore to the scene they were expecting a fully-armed assault party of fifth columnists. Instead, they found three startled beetle-hunters!

Ted talked to the Reverend Chalcraft about religion, too, and said his philosophy was best expressed in a poem he had written in 1976 for his old friend, the author and farmer Adrian Bell. It is entitled *Fulfilment*:

> Deep in the pool of life all wonders sleep,
> Yet at a touch are summoned to disport,
> Full-sensed and yielding gaily to the will
> That lures them from the silence and the gloom.
>
> Like winking bubbles in a glass they rise,
> All iridescent, leaping to be free
> And every moment changing their design:
> A destiny in every random gleam.
>
> So butterflies are born to brave the air,
> As pastel poplars grace the flowing breeze;
> As dolphins arc and dive in ecstasy
> And children run upon the sands in glee.
>
> But for the burning genius of the sun,
> The pale moon's Cupid glance upon the earth
> And every rhythm pulsed from farther space,
> Creation's sweet fulfilment had not come.
>
> When memory's eye looks down the aisles of Time,
> Let golden dreams dissolve the mists of grief;
> When, in the shadow and the light, the years
> Will wake and pass in beauty, one by one.
>
> Like daffodils the young friends dance again;
> Love's roses linger in the summer dusk;
> Glowing the harvest where ripe wisdom dwells
> And innocent December's quiet farewell.

There were hopes that the operation had been successful and, on Saturday 28 June, he came home. 'We then had a wonderful fortnight's weather,' says Phyllis. 'He sat outside and was even able to walk in the woods as far as the *machan* about a quarter of a mile away . . . We had lots and lots of visitors.'

He was still enthusiastic enough to stand by a tree for half an hour one day with Dr Roy Baker, puzzling over the identity of the creature which had left a trail of small holes up the bark. They eventually decided it must have been a tree-creeper. Dr Baker remembers that Ted was also curious about the effects of different types of soil on the colour of his rhododendrons, and was discussing some research they hoped to do together on black slugs — those little heroes of his first 'In the Country' article way back in 1946.

The Reverend Chalcraft visited him again, this time impulsively taking a John Betjeman poem, *Churchyards*. 'He would not let me read it to him — but took the book and read it aloud to me. It took quite some time.' The phone was constantly ringing with well-wishers. Other visitors were coming in and out. Ted interrupted his reading to say that the style of his own poems had sometimes been compared to Betjeman's. He interrupted himself again to show the vicar some photographs of beautiful lichens he had found growing on churchyard stones. Finally, he reached the last verse, and began to cry. 'He just put the book down and said — "Yes, that's it". I can't say more than that,' says the Reverend Chalcraft. 'It would be wrong of me to interpret.' That verse of the Betjeman poem reads:

> And, if it's true, no end is death.
> Mid-Lent is passed and Easter's near
> The greatest day of all the year
> When Jesus, who indeed had died,
> Rose with his body glorified.
> And if you find believing hard
> The primroses in your churchyard
> And modern science too will show
> That all things change the while they grow,
> And we, who change in Time will be
> Still more changed by Eternity.

By Thursday 10 July Ted was obviously not convalescent, as they had hoped; he was far from well. But he continued to get up, shave and go to his desk each day — still typing articles for the *EDP* until 14 July . . . and in that last article, published on 15 July, still learning from one of his readers:

Today I received for the first time a light hairy wolf-spider attacked by three small scarlet mites. . . .

Ted was taken back into hospital on Thursday 17 July, and died on the morning of the following Tuesday.

Two months later the Norfolk Naturalists Trust, and the Norfolk and Norwich Naturalists Society jointly awarded him the first-ever Sydney Long Memorial Medal to mark his 'unique knowledge of natural history in Norfolk'. Fittingly, it was a medal that had been created in honour of one of his old teachers — the same Dr Long who first took him bird-watching at Scolt Head Island.

The funeral on 28 July at St Mary's parish church, Surlingham, was conducted as a celebration. By request, no-one wore black. Phyllis, as every Sunday, played the organ and, this time, was accompanied by other members of the family, including two of their grandchildren — Rose playing the clarinet, and Polly playing the trumpet. It was the simple, village funeral Ted had asked for. But the church was decorated with wild flowers of the fen and the family made sure that they included one of his unlikely favourites . . . stinging nettles! At the graveside, medieval madrigals were played on violins and recorders and Mary read part of his poem *Fulfilment*.

Half a mile from the parish church, along a grassy track, stand the ruins of another church, St Saviour's. They are on a small hill which overlooks the Yare Valley, a bird sanctuary, and a broad sweep of fenland. As you look up the valley towards Norwich, the only building visible is the spire of Norwich Cathedral. There, at St Saviour's, Ted Ellis is buried — the first new grave since the eighteenth century.

Then, on 31 October, there was a second service at Norwich Cathedral — the contrast in scale illustrating the two lives of Ted Ellis, a simple man with an international reputation. His children and friends still played music but this time, the congregation consisted of more than 800 friends, dignitaries and eminent scientists from all over the world paying tribute. The clergy wore scarlet — the colour of celebration — for a service of thanksgiving.

Ted's eight grandchildren enjoy an afternoon at Wheatfen — *left to right* they are: Rose, Polly, Tom, Jesse, Emily, Richard, Matthew and Clare

151

11 🙟 The legacy

he programme of Ted's thanksgiving service — designed by his daughter Suzie — contained a hidden joke in its motif of a heron. The Norfolk 'harnser', no infrequent visitor to Wheatfen, had often been chosen by Arthur Patterson when, as a cartoonist, he caricatured his long-necked, sharp-featured, teenage protégé on letters and postcards. The heron has been chosen as symbol for the Ted Ellis Trust. For no story of Ted can end in death. Even as his family gathered at Wheatfen after the funeral, the idea of a Trust was born . . . to buy the land, care for it and make of it a permanent, living memorial.

Phyllis threw her energies into the project: fund raising, making a series of radio broadcasts of Ted's writings, and becoming a popular public speaker in her own right. Three trustees — Keith Clarke, Roy Baker and David Pearce-Gould — have announced an appeal for £120,000 to buy a hundred acres of the reedbeds, tidal channels and alder carrs, most of that money being needed to maintain it and build a small nature centre. The land is being sold to the Trust at a fraction of its private value in order to safeguard its future. David Bellamy officially launched the appeal in November 1987, but by then over £80,000 had already been raised, much of it in small £1 or £5 donations from ordinary families who wanted to pay tribute to the man they only knew through 'that lovely smile' on television. A separate 'Friends of the Ted Ellis Nature Reserve' group was formed, holding its first meeting in March 1988, to provide an opportunity for those who do not necessarily have special knowledge of natural history to become involved in the future of Wheatfen. And a book, *Ted Ellis's Year* — containing a selection of his writings for 1947 — was republished by the *EDP* in aid of the Trust.

At Wheatfen, the studying and recording did not stop for a day when Ted died. Other work is beginning too, including the cataloguing of his library of over 4,000 books, and the indexing — eventually for transfer onto computer — of his massive collection of 18,000 slides.

The Trust's aim is to keep the land just as Ted said to John Mountford — to 'look after it without looking after it', maintaining it sufficiently to prevent the gradual invasion of sallow and guelder-rose scrub but not 'tidying up' its variety. Wheatfen was always a deliberately untidy place. There were trees there which had not been touched since Ted first came; as they fell, so they were left to rot, becoming homes for insects and hosts for rare fungi. Not every part was quite so deliberately 'neglected'. He kept a lookout for rarities, for example, marking the position of especially precious plants with red-tagged stakes, and he positively protected the variety of small areas. For the value of Wheatfen is its diversity — as Ted realised on that first, amazed day as he walked around it with Captain Cockle.

Every type of countryside has its own special mixture of trees, plants, insects, birds, fish, fungi, and smaller lives which depend upon each other, providing rich interest to the specialist. Wheatfen is unusual for the number of distinct habitats within its 150 acres. But it has something more. Just because of its haphazard untidiness, these various habitats criss-cross, overlap and border each other in a patchwork confusion. Its layout defies all order and, wherever two habitats touch, that meeting creates a borderland habitat with its own special features. Adding further to the area's rarity is that it is freshwater — but tidal. The fens on the Yare are the only ones in Norfolk where water rises and falls regularly, providing frequent soaking but also allowing regular aeration of the matted floor of old plant remains inhabited by so many organisms of special interest such as the wetland slug.

The area from Rockland Broad, including Wheatfen, and as far as Cold-ham has been designated not only as a Site of Special Scientific Interest by the Nature Conservancy Council, but as one of their 'one-starred' sites — indicating its special status even among SSSIs.

'In the spirit of Ted's ideals,' said the trustees in a Norfolk and Norwich Naturalists Society bulletin, 'We hope to create at Wheatfen not a bird reserve or a nature reserve but a reserve for naturalists.' Thus, while doing as little as possible to it, the aim is to make it available for study — to the amateur as well as the professional, the schoolchild as well as the established naturalist. While details of its use remain to be settled by the Trust, the plan is to encourage, welcome and co-ordinate those specialists who will keep up the recording which has gone on there since Russell's first recollections and Captain Cockle's first card file. At the same time, it is hoped to make the fen available as an education centre for school parties — something always close to Ted and Phyllis's hearts.

As Roy Baker says: 'Ted wanted people to come here to study — or even just to wander — not to be given a brochure which points out, for example, "This is where a squirrel once sat". He wanted people to enjoy the experience of going out and looking around, observing, feeling the excitement!' Keith Clarke concurs with this and adds: 'Ted did not like the idea of going to a certain area, and dragooning nature — to produce, for example, a "typical reedbed" or any other "typical" habitat. He preferred a more

153

Top left: pointing the way ahead! Ted is pictured opening the 'Ted Ellis Way', a riverside walk to Fingringhoe, Essex. *Top right:* he presents conservation awards

David Bellamy the naturalist — here with Clare — is patron of the Trust

careful management in which you would frequently go out and do little bits of work, but would be interested in how nature was managing itself. Nature, of course, is a terrible conservationist! But provided you go out often enough, you can have a sort of "guided wilderness"'.

And so the legacy of Ted Ellis will take a lot of hard work — and will probably always depend on skilled parties of voluntary workers to provide the labour-intensive care required.

But perhaps one special part of the Ted Ellis legacy can only be preserved in his writings. That is the way in which he conveys to us the feeling that, however much he learned about Wheatfen, he still saw not facts, not even habitats . . . but 'magic' . . .

> Scientists may picture it all as a fantastic interplay of protons and neutrons jigging in Brownian movement, but the geological record tells a richer story of imagination and experimental enterprise that has been pulsing in the motes and threads of life on earth. We cannot believe in the fairyland of Shakespeare's 'Midsummer Night's Dream', but lacewings and hovering, darting bee-flies are just as magical and it is a fact that snails were using Cupid's darts in courtship even before our ancestral shrews were squeaking around in a world of dinosaurs.

It seems fitting, therefore, to end his story where it began — with words of encouragement to the young, just as Ted himself was encouraged in days long ago when, as a small boy in Guernsey, he embarked on his magical journey of fulfilment. This time, however, those words of encouragement are his own . . .

TO A CHILD
before it is too late

> Pass swiftly through this land: enter the forest: drink of springs: look up and far. The pigeons circle gladly, light on their wings. In the morning you shall see cheerful faces and join with those who trip and sing. Let snow fall, yet you may come where holly berries grow and ivy trails. There is a breeze: stir with the lake reeds and hillside pines, else may the jewelled bird outlive you in his joy.

> Spirit in the Way, know thou thy beauty, and out of the night, winged on the dawn, laughing to turrets of the golden clouds, kiss stars to sleep.

> Speed bright thoughts on mystery journeys. Now I see the way; swallow, thou see'st it; Sun, thou show'st it; now there is mist, but mist is of the sun, too.

> Ever is far, life no pale dream and death no rest. Earth moves: another life arises. This way and that light glances, winds blow.

> In the setting sun the waves, afire, leap on towards the shore, and daring to end — spent in that ecstasy — pause only while their frothy bubbles wink, then to the tide return.

Norfolk and Norwich
Naturalists' Society
FOUNDED 1869

SYDNEY LONG
MEMORIAL MEDAL

Dr. Ted Ellis devoted his life and his extraordinary talents as a field naturalist to the well-being of and research into Norfolk's wildlife.

As a young protege of Arthur Paterson he acquired further knowledge and sympathy for the County's wildlife in the Natural History Department at the Museum between 1928 and 1956. His honorary Doctorate was conferred by the University of East Anglia in 1970.

His unique capacity to communicate and inspire interest in wildlife was only matched by his scholarly and often original research into all aspects of the County's Natural History.

In the opinion of the Councils of the Norfolk Naturalists Trust and the Norfolk and Norwich Naturalists' Society, Dr. Ted Ellis's contribution to our knowledge of the natural history of Norfolk is unique and his example to existing and future generations of Norfolk people beyond praise.

1986

Postscript

by Phyllis Ellis

Eugene Stone never knew Ted; neither did he know the Ellis family until after Ted had died; but now that he has met its members, chased over the countryside to meet our friends, and, above all, read the countless thousands of words in forty years' worth of 'Countrysides', it seems to me that he sees Ted and life at Wheatfen more clearly than we who lived it.

So many, many friends could not be met, written to or consulted about this life story — how many facets there are we have not touched! How many societies he joined and helped! President of Norwich Sub Aqua Club (but couldn't swim!), President of the Morris Men, but really had two left feet in spite of a good sense of rhythm — no man could so easily produce mayhem in the *Dashing White Sergeant!*

He was everybody's friend on television. I cannot say how many people greeted us in the street as well-known and loved friends (not just acquaintances) though they had never before seen him in the flesh! People addressed their envelopes to 'The People's Naturalist' and that was what he was. Strangers come up to me now and say 'He had such a lovely smile!'

We may be criticised that this is a biography of omissions. I do not know enough to analyse his scientific work or worth; it was undoubtedly valuable as he was rewarded for it with an honorary doctorate — the climax, in one way, of his aspirations, and an unforgettable and totally unexpected peak in his life. As Tim Wyatt says, life with Ted was not always lived peacefully, but upsets, while noisy, were never long lasting and no grudges were borne.

There has been no room to mention by name so many people who have helped us during our married life — people like Freda Hayhow who, for over thirty years has coped with the household difficulties . . . Ted's piles of books, gumboots on polished floors, the old, the young and, of course, Ted himself. I would like to thank Freda. I could never have done all I did without her help. And I would like to thank, with all my heart, all our hundreds of friends who have given me so much support in the last two busy years. The Ted Ellis Trust is safely off the ground, although we need more support to complete our aim of a nature centre here; and, of course, we do need more 'Friends of the Ted Ellis Nature Reserve', as well. Please let me know if you are interested. I still live at Wheatfen.

The Ted Ellis Trust

For Ted Ellis, life was an adventure. We hope that for many people this book, too, will be in some way a beginning.

Help is needed; gifts and services of all kinds would be welcomed by the Ted Ellis Trust which has already begun the task of looking after Wheatfen Broad, one of the most fascinating areas of scientific interest in the country.

One very practical and enjoyable way of contributing is by joining the Friends of the Ted Ellis Trust. The Friends meet socially from time to time, receive the Trust's regular newsletter, and visit Wheatfen at various seasons of the year. By September 1988, there were nearly 600 members and if you would like to join, please send your name and address to Phyllis Ellis at Wheatfen Broad, Surlingham, Norwich NR14 7AL, along with a £5 annual subscription for individuals or £10 for family membership.

During 1988, the Trust became registered as a charity. Progress has been made to make the area more accessible — particularly to disabled visitors, with a levelled path negotiable by wheelchairs. The Trust say that this is one of their main aims: 'We want to preserve it, but we want it to be a place for everyone to enjoy. For the handicapped in particular it has a great deal to offer and that is why we are doing our best to make it accessible to them as far as we possibly can.'

For the physically fit, a two and a half mile round walk has been created. Visitors in 1988 included scouts, guides and children with special learning difficulties. Phyllis commented: 'In many nature reserves — quite rightly, since they have thousands of visitors each year — children are not allowed to stray off the paths. But it seems to me sad that there are children between seven and ten who have never had the opportunity to climb a tree. At Wheatfen, we are able to let them play, climb trees and explore in a wild area — allowing them a natural approach to discovering nature.'

Children have also been involved, alongside adults, in conservation work — helping to protect a rich and fragile ecology from invasion by sallow and guelder rose scrub, thus preserving something which we can all enjoy for many years to come.

About the author

Eugene Stone was born in London in 1951 and worked as a journalist in Essex and East London, before coming to Norwich in 1981, where he took a degree at the University of East Anglia. He is now a freelance writer with a strong interest in environmental issues, mental health and education. *Ted Ellis – The People's Naturalist* is his first book.

Picture Credits

Pictures appearing in this book are used by kind permission of Phyllis Ellis, Anglia Television, the BBC, Radio Times, Eastern Daily Press, Norwich Castle Museum, Mr R. Robinson, Norfolk Naturalists Trust and Suzie Hanna; pictures by J.G. Wilson, A. Millard and John Markham are also included.